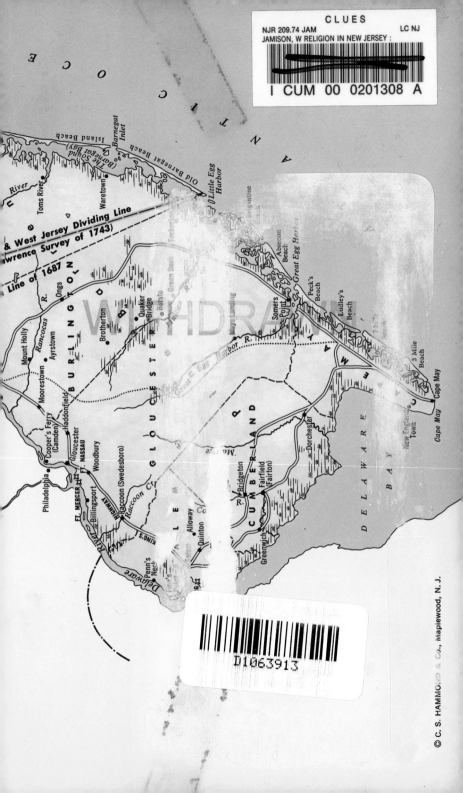

Religion in New Jersey:
A Brief History

THE NEW JERSEY HISTORICAL SERIES

Edited by

RICHARD M. HUBER   WHEATON J. LANE

Volume 13

The New Jersey Historical Series

Religion in New Jersey:

A Brief History

WALLACE N. JAMISON

1964

D. VAN NOSTRAND COMPANY, INC.

Princeton, New Jersey

New York, N. Y. • Toronto, Canada • London, England

D. VAN NOSTRAND COMPANY, INC.
120 Alexander St., Princeton, New Jersey (*Principal office*)
24 West 40 Street, New York 18, New York

D. VAN NOSTRAND COMPANY, LTD.
358, Kensington High Street, London, W.14, England

D. VAN NOSTRAND COMPANY (*Canada*), LTD.
25 Hollinger Road, Toronto 16, Canada

Published simultaneously in Canada by
D. VAN NOSTRAND COMPANY (Canada), LTD.

PRINTED IN THE UNITED STATES OF AMERICA

To KATHY and BOB

. . . who will continue the story

FOREWORD

Many tracks will be left by the New Jersey Tercentenary celebration, but few will be larger than those made by the New Jersey Historical Series. The Series is a monumental publishing project the product of a remarkable collaborative effort between public and private enterprise.

New Jersey has needed a series of books about itself. The 300th anniversary of the State is a fitting time to publish such a series. It is to the credit of the State's Tercentenary Commission that this series has been created.

In an enterprise of such scope, there must be many contributors. Each of these must give considerably of himself if the enterprise is to succeed. The New Jersey Historical Series, the most ambitious publishing venture ever undertaken about a state, was conceived by a committee of Jerseymen—Julian P. Boyd, Wesley Frank Craven, John T. Cunningham, David S. Davies, and Richard P. McCormick. Not only did these men outline the need for such an historic venture; they also aided in the selection of the editors of the series.

Both jobs were well done. The volumes speak for themselves. The devoted and scholarly services of Richard M. Huber and Wheaton J. Lane, the editors, are a part of every book in the series. The editors have been aided in their work by two fine assistants, Elizabeth Jackson Holland and Bertha DeGraw Miller.

To D. Van Nostrand Company, Inc. my special thanks for recognizing New Jersey's need and for bringing their skills and publishing wisdom to bear upon the printing and distributing of the New Jersey Historical Series.

My final and most heartfelt thanks must go to Wallace N. Jamison, who accepted my invitation to write *Religion in New Jersey: A Brief History,* doing so at great personal sacrifice and without thought of material gain. We are richer by his scholarship. We welcome this important contribution to an understanding of our State.

RICHARD J. HUGHES
*Governor of the
State of New Jersey*

January, 1964

PREFACE

No history of a people is complete until careful attention has been given to its religious beliefs and practices. Particularly is this true of the people who originally settled New Jersey, for most of them came there either to escape religious persecution in their homeland or to find a greater freedom to practice their faith according to the dictates of their conscience.

A volume of this size can do little more than suggest the outlines of the story and trace its most significant movements. An attempt has been made throughout to paint the picture with fairly broad strokes. For the readers who wish more information on a favorite denomination or locality, it is hoped that the bibliographical note at the end of this volume will provide suggestions for further reading.

This book would not have been possible without the generous assistance of many church leaders, librarians, and historians. Space does not permit giving full credit to all of them by name, but a number have been outstanding in their offers of time and good counsel. Mr. Donald A. Sinclair, Curator of the Special Collections Department of Rutgers University Library, and the Reverend Peter N. VandenBerge, Librarian of the Gardner A. Sage Library of New Brunswick Theological Library, were extremely helpful in making available their collections of early source materials. The General Editors of the Tercentenary Series, Dr. Richard M. Huber and Dr. Wheaton J. Lane have been most gracious in supplying critical comments as the work progressed. The number of errors in fact and omissions in detail has been materially decreased by the careful reading of the whole work by Dr. Nelson R. Burr, the Reverend Thomas J. Frain, Dr. Robert T. Handy, Dr. Lefferts Loetscher, and the Reverend Alexander Hamilton Shaw. Whatever faults remain are, of course, the sole responsibility of the author. Finally, a word of thanks is due to Mrs. Beatrice Cook who spent late hours in preparing the manuscript for the publisher.

WALLACE N. JAMISON

New Brunswick, New Jersey
January, 1964

x

TABLE OF CONTENTS

LIST OF ILLUSTRATIONS

INTRODUCTION

If WE DEFINE RELIGION as the attempt to relate human beings to that which is divine, then the history of religion in any one place must begin with the first human inhabitants. All societies of which we have any knowledge have exhibited in one way or another this concern for the divine. Through sacrifices, prayers, sacred rites and rituals men have tried in myriad ways to draw near to God to secure His favor. Since the earliest inhabitants of New Jersey, so far as we know, were American Indians, the history of religion should begin with them. The particular tribe that lived in New Jersey when the white man first made his appearance here, was the Lenni Lenape or Delaware Indians. They belonged to the great Algonquin family which stretched along much of the Atlantic seaboard. Apparently they moved about a great deal, and at no time was there a large number of them in New Jersey. According to William Penn, "Their Worship consists of two parts, Sacrifice and *Cantico*. Their Sacrifice is their first Fruits; the first and fattest buck they kill, goeth to the fire, where he is all burnt with a Mournful Ditty of him that performeth the Ceremony. . . . The other part is their *Cantico*, performed by round-Dances, sometimes Words, sometimes Songs." * A little later, a Welsh Quaker by the name of Gabriel Thomas wrote of the

* Letter from William Penn to the Committee of the Free Societies of Traders, 1683 as found in A. C. Myers (ed.), *Narratives of Early Pennsylvania, West New Jersey and Delaware 1630-1707* (New York, 1912), 234.

Indians, "They observe New Moons, they offer their first Fruits to a *Maneto*, or suppos'd Deity, whereof they have two, one, as they fansie, above (good), another below (bad), and have a kind of Feast of Tabernacles, laying their Altars upon Twelve Stones, observe a sort of Mourning twelve Months, Customs of Women, and many other Rites." *

Like most of the other Indian tribes, the Lenni Lenape believed in a life after death where the spirits lived with a Great King somewhere to the "South." To prepare the dead for the next life, they were buried surrounded by their weapons and tools as well as food and wampum for the journey. Artifacts from these graves have been recovered in considerable numbers as old burial grounds were ploughed up by the white settlers. Today the Indian is remembered in New Jersey because of the place names he left us, such as Rahway, Passaic, Raritan, Watchung, Pompton, Hackensack, and many more,** but his religion had no effect whatever on the European invaders who displaced him.

The white men began to arrive and start settlements early in the seventeenth century. From that point on a new religious history began, one which had its roots not in the New World but in the Old. On looking at a map of New Jersey, it might be supposed that the state would rapidly develop a society that was fairly homogeneous in character. After all, it is a fairly small state,† and it has very clearly defined boundaries on all but a portion of its northern perimeter. Yet, curiously, New Jersey was one of the last colonies to develop any clear image of itself. Indeed, the history of New Jersey might be described as

* Gabriel Thomas, "An Historical and Geographical Account of the Province and Country of Pensilvania and of West-New-Jersey in America," 1698, in *Narratives of Early Pennsylvania, West New Jersey and Delaware, 1630-1707* (New York, 1912), 315. See also *Proceedings of The New Jersey Historical Society*, VIII, No. 1, 3ff.

** See Charles F. Philhower, "The Original Inhabitants of Union County," *Proceedings of The New Jersey Historical Society*, VIII, No. 2, 124-138.

† Of the thirteen original colonies, only three, Connecticut, Delaware, and Rhode Island, were smaller in land area.

the story of a state in search of its own identity. Unlike the clear Puritan image of Massachusetts or the plantation image of Virginia, New Jersey was a state without a face. Or, at best, it was a state with many faces. This general observation holds true for the religious life of the state as much as for its politics and economics. For one thing, settlers came to New Jersey in fewer numbers and at a later date than they did to the colonies around them. When New York and Philadelphia were thriving cities, much of New Jersey was still uninhabited. Nowhere along its coast was there a natural harbor that could rival these two great ports. The central part of the state was heavily wooded so that travel was difficult and in addition much of the rest of the land was not attractive for farming. No wonder that the early proprietors had a difficult time finding families who would settle there.

In addition to the geographical difficulties which confronted the settler, the hazards of history soon divided the colony in two when James, Duke of York, gave the territory to two of his close friends, John, Lord Berkeley and Sir George Carteret. When Berkeley decided to sell his share, they drew a more or less arbitrary line running northwest and southeast, setting up two proprietary colonies which made social unity most unlikely. It became even more unlikely when a group of Quakers bought out Lord Berkeley and proceeded to make West Jersey a haven for English Friends. While West Jersey, as a result, achieved some degree of uniformity, East Jersey from the start was made up of a wide diversity of religious and social groups—English, Scots, Irish, Welsh, French Huguenots, Dutch Reformed, Presbyterians, Congregationalists, Baptists, German Lutherans, Moravians, and a number more. Even in West Jersey other religious groups, such as the Baptists and Lutherans, penetrated, so that religious hegemony there was never complete. Paradoxically, religion in any society can be both a unifying influence and a divisive one. Whenever the society creates a state church, then the religion embodied in that church can have a powerful unifying effect. Since this was the pattern of most of the European states, the American colonies were not long in following their example. But New Jersey, like Rhode Island, Pennsylvania, and Delaware, never established a state church.

As a consequence, religion was apt to become disruptive. A number of the early colonial citizens regarded the religious diversity of the state as a sign of irreligion. Actually, it was nothing of the kind. Instead it was a collection of widely diverse religious groups trying to learn how to live in community. The results, while painful at times, were also surprising, even to those who were involved. They discovered that religious diversity was possible within a framework of political unity. They also learned, when vital social and religious movements such as the Great Awakening and later the abolitionist crusade swept across the land, that denominational lines were ineffective to distinguish various kinds of Christians. Revivalism was apt to make a Presbyterian pastor feel closer kinship with a Methodist preacher than with his own brethren in his church. From this diversity in New Jersey came a spirit, at least on the lay level, of broad tolerance, of "live-and-let-live" which became characteristic of the entire Union by the time of the Civil War. Thus New Jersey helped provide the experience out of which came the doctrine of separation of church and state which has been a key policy of our national life. Instead of fighting one another all the time (which also happened), the citizens of New Jersey learned how to tap the riches preserved in each denominational heritage. As one historian has fittingly observed:

Before the end of the seventeenth century, these two provinces (East and West Jersey) displayed a variety of nationalities and religious beliefs hardly rivalled by any other colony in America. New Jersey was an early sample of the present American religious diversity. Here were found the pacifism and acute social conscience of the Friends; the civic pride and educational zeal of the New England Puritan, the Scottish Presbyterian, and the Dutch Calvinist; the Baptist's ardent toleration and opposition to a state church; the Anglican's devotion to the Prayer Book; the sound liturgical and doctrinal traditions of the Swedish Lutherans; and the prophetic and emotional

warmth of the minor sects, the forerunners of our modern
Pentecostal and similar denominations.*

What appeared at first to be a divisive and chaotic multiplicity of sects has proved in the end to be both enrich-
ing and unifying to the citizenry of our State.

If diversity is one key to the religious history of New
Jersey, the other and more serious one is polarity. As has
already been mentioned, the settlement of the state was
relatively slow. New York and Philadelphia rapidly out-
stripped Perth Amboy and Burlington. Since the former
were thriving commercial centers, they attracted settlers,
accumulated wealth and political power. It was not long
until New Jersey was divided by the two cities near its
northern and southern extremities. As the poles of a
great magnet organize the metal fragments surrounding
them, so the port cities soon came to orient the cultural
life of the areas surrounding them. New Jersey became
polarized between the two. This had as profound an
effect on the religious development of New Jersey as it
had on politics and economics. For reasons which cannot
be explored too deeply here, New York usually became
the center of liberalism, whereas Philadelphia's orientation was more conservative. In part it was caused by the
diversity of New York's religious affiliations, by the ab-
sorption of radical European ideas in its schools and
colleges, and by its easy tolerance for differences of
opinion without which its polyglot population could
never have continued as a political unit. Philadelphia, on
the other hand, for most of the colonial era was under
the dominance of wealthy Quaker families who were
quite conservative religiously. While the Friends were
tolerant of other faiths, within their own fellowship they
soon became fairly rigid as the Keithian and Hicksite
revolts illustrate. This general conservative frame of
mind seems to have affected the other religious groups
in the area as well. As denominations spread across the
state, this urban polarization was bound to produce fric-

* Nelson R. Burr, *The Anglican Church in New Jersey* (Philadelphia, 1954), 3, 4.

tion between northern liberals and southern conservatives. The classic example of this is found in the history of the Presbyterian Church, but the same influences operated among the Quakers, the Lutherans, the Baptists, and, to a certain extent, among the Methodists as well. The Episcopalians prove a curious exception to this influence. While they had liberal and conservative branches, the northern part was the more conservative and the southern more liberal, but this was brought about by political concerns which will be dealt with later. Even the Roman Catholic Church shows some signs of being affected by this polarizing influence, though it was affected less and overcame it sooner than its Protestant neighbors.

Up to the middle of the twentieth century the tension within the various denominations produced by the interaction of the New York-influenced and Philadelphia-influenced branches periodically broke into violent dispute and at times schism. Even when this was not the case, there was an underlying suspicion which was a constant hazard to denominational peace, if not unity. Within the last few decades, however, a whole gamut of new influences with centers outside of New York and Philadelphia has come into play with the result that the old tensions no longer occupy the important place they once did. The ecumenical movement with its world-wide sweep, the union of denominations with centers in the midwest, the growing dialogue between Protestant and Catholic have created an atmosphere in which the old liberal-conservative battle seems largely irrelevant.

This, then, is the story of how the people of one state, New Jersey, have sought to discover their religious identity. It is an account of ludicrous acts as well as heroic ones, of ignoble deeds as well as fine. Though the story has not ended and must therefore be incomplete, it is possible to see certain lines of achievement during the last three centuries which indicate that the religious struggles of the past were not without their value and that what our fathers wrought was not wrought in vain.

I

THE MUCH PROMISED LAND
1620-1702

T HE GREAT LAND GRAB which European countries conducted during the seventeenth century affected the future
state of New Jersey even more than the other colonies.
The Dutch, Swedes, and English all sought to secure
territory for colonization there. Since possession is eleven
points in the law, each kingdom sought to encourage
emigration to its colonies by every inducement and
promise possible. As a consequence New Jersey was
offered to so many groups and was bound up with so
many concessions that it could well be called the much-
promised land.

Even though the English laid general claim to the
eastern seaboard from Maine to the Carolinas, it was the
Dutch who first began settlement in Manhattan in 1621,
and seventeen years later the Swedes followed with a
settlement along the Delaware. It was from the Dutch
settlement that the first attempt came to occupy New
Jersey by the white man. Dutch farmers crossed the Hudson to cultivate the land in a territory called Pavonia.*
Land was purchased from the Indians and farms were
settled, but repeated friction with neighboring tribes and
resulting massacres prevented any permanent settlement
until the town of Bergen was laid out in 1660. Because
of the scattered nature of the Dutch settlements west of
the Hudson, no attempt was made at first to organize a

* See John E. Pomfret, *The Province of East New Jersey, 1609-
1702* (Princeton, 1962), Chapter I.

church. Aside from the occasional visit of a traveling dominie, New Jersey farmers had to make a trip to Manhattan to share in the services of the Dutch Reformed Church.

Meanwhile, far to the south, the Swedes began a settlement along the Delaware River. They established a string of forts on the west bank, and this aroused the Dutch whose settlement at Fort Nassau below the present site of Camden guarded the interests of the Dutch West India Company in west Jersey. It was not until 1643, however, that the Swedes began settling on the Jersey side. Governor Johan Printz, the corpulent leader of the Swedes whom the Indians called "Big Tub," set about establishing two forts to protect the settlement of Christina (near modern Wilmington). These forts on the Jersey side encouraged Swedish settlers to stake out farms nearby so that in the next few years there was a generous sprinkling of Swedes concentrated near Raccoon (later Swedesboro) and Penn's Neck (now Churchtown). At first these Swedish Lutherans were served by pastors who lived on the other side of the Delaware, though for seven months a Lutheran minister, Israel Holgh Fluviander, resided at Fort Elfsborg, a few miles south of Salem. To him must go the honor of being the first resident clergyman in New Jersey, even though his tenure set something of a record for brevity.*

While the Swedish colony, as such, ceased to exist after the Dutch conquest of 1655, a succession of Lutheran pastors continued to serve the scattered Swedes of Gloucester County until late in the eighteenth century when most of the Swedes were assimilated into the Society of Friends or the German Lutheran congregations.**

* Nelson R. Burr, "The Religious History of New Jersey Before 1702," *Proceedings of The New Jersey Historical Society*, LVI, No. 3, 171ff. See John E. Pomfret, *The Province of East New Jersey, 1609-1702* (Princeton, 1962), 23.

** Nicholas Collin, "A Brief Account of the Swedish Mission in Racoon [sic] and Penn's Neck, New Jersey," *Proceedings of The New Jersey Historical Society*, III, No. 3, 105-122. See also S. H. Richards, "New Stockholm—The Swedish Settlement," *Proceedings of The New Jersey Historical Society*, XV, No. 4, 487-502.

The Dutch control of the area was short lived, however. In 1664 a British fleet appeared off the tip of Manhattan Island and demanded the surrender of the Dutch garrison. Governor Peter Stuyvesant was furious and wanted to fight it out to the last man which, considering the rather sorry state of his defenses, would not have taken long. His colleagues, on the other hand, saw the uselessness of resistance and so urged a subordination of patriotism to common sense. In the end, Stuyvesant surrendered without a struggle, and the British took over the control of all Dutch territories in the New World. Meanwhile King Charles II had already issued a patent conferring on his brother James, Duke of York, title to Long Island, Manhattan, and all the territory between there and the Delaware River. In turn, James granted the Jersey land to two of his close friends, John, Lord Berkeley and Sir George Carteret. This newly created province was given the name *Nova Caesarea,* or New Jersey, in honor of Sir George who had been governor of the Isle of Jersey during the English Civil War and had protected it from the Puritans.

Up to this time, aside from the small Dutch settlement around Bergen and the Swedish settlements in Gloucester County, the land was inhabited only by Indian tribes. Much of it was heavily wooded and uninviting for a number of reasons. Regarding one settlement in south Jersey, an early historian remarked, "The Musketoes were so numerous, the Swedes were unable to live here, and therefore removing, named the place, Musketoeburgh." * Many a latter-day south Jerseyman has had reason to comment on the propriety of that name.

FOUNDATIONS OF RELIGIOUS LIBERTY

Since both Berkeley and Carteret were eager to realize some income from their holdings, they set about to encourage colonization. Accordingly they drew up a series

* Samuel Smith, *The History of the Colony of Nova-Caesaria or New Jersey* (2nd ed.; Burlington, 1877), 24, 25.

of Concessions and Agreements which were designed to make settlement in their province as attractive as possible. They were shrewd enough to realize that many of the men who left England to settle in the New World did so to escape an oppressive religious establishment. So the following concessions regarding religious belief and practice had an important place in their declaration:

No person qualified as aforesaid [freeman] within the said province, at any time shall be any ways molested, punished, disquieted or called in question, for any difference in opinion or practice in matters of religious concernments, who do not actually disturb the civil peace of the said province; but that all and every such person and persons, may, from time to time, and at all times, freely and fully have and enjoy his and their judgments and consciences, in matters of religion, throughout the said province, they behaving themselves peaceably and quietly, and not using this liberty to licentiousness, nor to the civil injury or outward disturbance of others.*

With the publication of the Concessions and Agreements, Berkeley and Carteret sat back to await the rush of settlers to their lands. Unhappily, the rush never materialized. George Fox, the Quaker leader, made a trip across New Jersey in 1672 and in his diary noted that "we have travelled a whole Day together without seeing Man of Woman, House or Dwelling place." ** It is true that there were a substantial number of Quakers in East Jersey at the time whom Fox also visited, and it may have been the account of his trip to William Penn which helped create an interest in the area as the site of a future Quaker colony.† Finally Lord Berkeley gave up hope of making a fortune from his proprietorship and sold his share to two Quakers, John Fenwick and Edward

* Samuel Smith, *The History of the Colony of Nova-Caesaria, or New Jersey* (2nd ed.; Burlington, 1877), Appendix I, 513.

** *The Journal of George Fox* (Cambridge, 1911), II, 434. See John E. Pomfret, *The Province of West New Jersey, 1609-1702* (Princeton, 1956), 61.

† Rufus M. Jones, *The Quakers in the American Colonies* (London, 1911), 359-362.

Byllynge, for £1000. This forced the division of the colony into two parts. Thereafter East New Jersey and West New Jersey were separated by a diagonal line which extended from the east side of Little Egg Harbor northwest to a point on the upper Delaware not far from the Delaware Water Gap. Despite the fact that both Fenwick and Byllynge became involved in financial difficulties and had to transfer title to some other Quakers, including William Penn, plans were made to start a Quaker colony in West New Jersey. In order to make the venture as attractive as possible, the proprietors worked out their own Concessions and Agreements which would establish the conditions of settlement. Unsurprisingly, religious toleration is given a prominent place in these provisions. Proceeding from the premise "that no man, nor number of men upon earth, hath power or authority to rule over men's consciences in religious matters . . ." the Concessions ruled that "every such person and persons, may . . . have and enjoy . . . the exercise of their consciences, in matters of religious worship throughout all the said province." * This document did much to establish the basis of church relations in New Jersey from that day to this and still stands as one of the finest statements of religious liberty anywhere.

The Quaker Commonwealth

From then on the colonization of the two divisions, East New Jersey and West New Jersey, proceeded in quite different ways. The latter, under Quaker auspices, maintained a more homogeneous character as William Penn and his friends tried to carry out their plans "to show Quakerism at work, freed from hampering conditions." ** Thus while the Eastern division attracted settlers as a frank means of turning a quick profit, the Friends

* Samuel Smith, *The History of the Colony of Nova-Caesaria, or New Jersey* (2nd ed.; Burlington, 1877), Appendix II, 529.
** Rufus M. Jones, *The Quakers in the American Colonies* (London, 1911), 357.

in the Western division were more concerned with the establishment of a just and godly society in line with the tenets of their faith. Accordingly, they screened prospective colonists to discourage the lazy or rebellious and encouraged the industrious. Skilled artisans were especially sought out and urged to settle in the Quaker colony. The earliest colonists had established friendly relations with the local Indians and were thus freed from the fear of Indian raids. Almost from the first the colony prospered. Within eighteen months of its founding in 1675, at least eight hundred Quakers sailed up the Delaware to land at Salem or Burlington and by 1681 there were fourteen hundred in West New Jersey.

The first religious services of the Friends were held in tents rigged from the sails of their ships. After houses had been built, the services of worship were conducted in the larger private homes. It was not long, however, before meetinghouses were erected first in Salem and then in Burlington.* The concern of these first colonists for regular and adequate worship was a natural consequence of the persecution they had undergone in the Old World. Of the 120 First Purchasers of proprieties in West Jersey more than a third had suffered imprisonment or fines for their Quaker convictions.** Without a question the primary reason for the emigration of many colonists to West New Jersey was the prospect of free worship even more than the inducement of cheap land and financial reward. Typical was the letter of an early Quaker colonist, Daniel Wills, to a friend in London:

When I am walking alone, and the sense of the Lord's good dealings is brought before me; I cannot but admire him for his mercies, and often in secret bless his name, that ever he turn'd my face hitherward, and gave me confidence in himself, and

* Rufus M. Jones, *The Quakers in the American Colonies* (London, 1911), 363-368.
** John E. Pomfret, *The Province of West New Jersey, 1609-1702* (Princeton, 1956), 119.

boldness by faith, to oppose all gainsayers; though never so strong.*

Even though West Jersey from the first was open to colonization by anyone willing to purchase land there regardless of faith or creed, the overwhelming majority of the colonists were Friends. As a consequence, the colony quickly established a fairly homogeneous character which was enforced by the Quaker organization. The pattern for this organization had been worked out by George Fox in England. The local meeting, which corresponded to a congregation in established churches, gathered for worship at least once a week or oftener. This group constituted itself as the Monthly Meeting to transact the necessary religious business of the community. The Monthly Meeting, which was the basic unit of organization, recorded the vital statistics of the group such as births, deaths, and marriages. It dismissed members to other meetings and received Friends who moved from other meetings to the area of its jurisdiction. The earliest monthly meeting was established at Salem in 1676 and another was formed at Burlington two years later.** One important duty of the monthly meeting was to enforce discipline, both social and moral, among its members. It decided when a member broke the rules of society and determined the punishment to be inflicted. Thus it served as an invaluable stabilizing force in the community.

As monthly meetings increased in number the Quarterly Meeting was organized. It was a delegated body consisting of a certain number of members from each monthly meeting in a given area who met together every three months. The Quarterly Meeting adjudicated between disputing monthly meetings or served as a court of appeal from the judgment of a monthly meeting. The

* Quoted in Samuel Smith, *The History of the Colony of Nova-Caesarea, or New Jersey* (2nd ed.; Burlington, 1877), 115.
** John E. Pomfret, *The Province of West New Jersey, 1609-1702* (Princeton, 1956), 217ff.

earliest Quarterly Meeting in America was the Burlington Quarterly Meeting which met for the first time in July, 1681, with Salem following a year later. The top judicatory in the Quaker system was the Yearly Meeting which established policy for a fairly widespread region often covering a number of colonies. The West Jersey Quaker settlements did not organize themselves into a Yearly Meeting until fairly late, apparently believing that all necessary policy-making decisions could be handled by the Quarterly Meetings. Finally, the Jersey Quakers became part of the Philadelphia Yearly Meeting which had a commanding voice for all Quakers in the Middle Colonies. The Yearly Meetings kept in close touch with the London Yearly Meeting through correspondence and thus the entire religious movement was bound together. Though life was not easy in any of the American colonies of the seventeenth century, West Jersey quietly prospered and remained at peace with its neighbors. The advance planning by the English Friends, the screening of prospective colonists so that only the serious-minded went, the broad toleration which was written into the Concessions and Agreements and the just treatment of the Indians insured a successful enterprise from the start.

East Jersey Puritanism

When Sir George Carteret died in 1679, the Proprietary Colony of East Jersey came up for sale. William Penn and eleven other Friends immediately sought to add it to their West Jersey holdings, and in 1681 the sale was consummated for £3000. Thus the Quakers assumed control of all New Jersey. Their dream of placing a Quaker stamp on the whole colony similar to that of West Jersey, however, was never realized. For one thing the forests and bogs which separated the two parts of the proprietorship made communications extremely difficult by land. But even more important, settlements had already sprung up in East Jersey that were not infrequently hostile to the Quaker beliefs. Whether time would have worked in favor of the Friends we cannot tell, because twenty years later they surrendered the government to Queen Anne of England and New Jersey became a Royal Colony.*

East Jersey by this time was a potpourri of settlements representing Congregationalists, Presbyterians, Baptists, Anglicans, and a few Quakers. By and large each settlement had its own dominant religious faith so that relations among settlements was never as close in East Jersey as they were in their neighboring colony to the southwest. One of the earliest East Jersey settlements was the town of Newark founded in 1666 by a group of settlers from Milford, Connecticut. They were English Congregationalists who decided to leave their Puritan colony in New England, not because life there was too severe, but because it was growing dangerously lax. The first Puritan settlers in New England were people of deep religious commitment who insisted that no one was eligible for church membership who had not received a personal experience of God's redeeming grace. This conversion experience had certain outward marks which could be noted by the congregation as a whole. So admission to the Lord's Table and church membership were dependent not only on a moral life and knowledge of the catechism and Scriptures but also on this conversion experience. With the passage of the years, fewer and fewer of the colonists qualified for admission to membership. The question then arose, were the children of baptized non-church members eligible for baptism? According to strict Puritan belief, they were not. But after much dissension the churches of New England approved the Half-Way Covenant, which allowed baptized colonists who had never been converted and received into full church membership to present their children for baptism.

The bitterness engendered by the debate over the Half-Way Covenant was so deep that some of the strict Puritans sought to break away and establish themselves elsewhere. Thus when the offer of land in East Jersey with

* Rufus M. Jones, *The Quakers in the American Colonies* (London, 1911), 363-368.

liberal concessions for self-government was made by the Duke of York, Puritans from Milford and New Haven came to start a new and more pure theocracy than was possible in New England. Unlike their predecessors in New England, these latter-day Puritans first purchased their land from the Indians and thus helped insure for East Jersey the same freedom from Indian wars which West Jersey enjoyed. At first the settlement was named Milford, but then the name was changed to Newark after Newark-on-Trent in England, the original home of their pastor, the Reverend Abraham Pierson.* Epitome of the stern Puritan divine, the Reverend Mr. Pierson had come from Branford, Connecticut, with his entire church organization and some additional settlers from nearby Guilford. Like his parishioners, he was a strict Calvinist who abominated compromises like the Half-Way Covenant. The worship of these people was almost devoid of liturgy, emphasizing rather simplicity of form and purity of doctrine. On the other hand, they resembled the New England Puritans in seeking a virtual identity of church and state. Both their clergy and meetinghouses were supported by an obligatory tax. Political authority and the vote were reserved for church members alone. "For more than fifty years the government of the town was essentially a government by and for its church." **

Other Congregational churches with only slightly less rigorous Calvinistic principles were founded at Elizabethtown and Woodbridge, the former being founded two years prior to Newark and the latter in 1675. For over fifty years the Puritan traditions of New England were nurtured in the Congregational churches established

* Nelson R. Burr, "The Religious History of New Jersey Before 1702" *Proceedings of The New Jersey Historical Society*, LVI, No. 3, 179. A less reliable tradition claims that Newark was named because it was to be the "New Ark of the Covenant." See W. T. Hanzsche, "The History of the Churches in New Jersey" in *The Story of New Jersey* (New York, 1945), II, 238 and Joseph Atkinson, *The History of Newark* (Newark, 1878), 12-20, 54.

** Walter S. Nichols, "Early Newark as a Puritan Theocracy in Colonial New Jersey," *Proceedings of The New Jersey Historical Society*, V, No. 4, 204.

in these communities. Their ministers, when they could get them, usually came from New England and had been educated at Harvard, or, later, at Yale. In addition there were substantial settlements of Puritans in Piscataway, Middletown, and Shrewsbury.* The chief difficulty encountered by the Puritan churches in Jersey was the securing of pastors. The Congregational clergy of New England were always reluctant to stray very far from Boston Commons, especially to churches where congregations were small and financial support uncertain. In one instance a Scottish minister who had fled the religious persecution in his homeland served as pastor of the Woodbridge congregation, but he stayed only until the persecution ended and then he returned to Scotland.

At first the Congregational churches supported their churches and clergy by a compulsory tax as was customary in New England. This was possible where all the residents of a town were Puritans, as in the case of Newark. But when a sizable proportion were of another faith this method of financing ran into trouble. Soon after Samuel Shepherd took the pulpit at Woodbridge, a Quaker by the name of William Webster refused to pay the portion of his tax that went toward the minister's salary. Shortly others followed suit with the result that the support of the minister by taxation had to be abandoned in 1700, and funds for this purpose were solicited by voluntary contribution.** In this way the Jersey churches were forced to give up the state-support pattern that characterized Britain and Europe for the voluntary support that became typical of all churches in America a few decades later.

Largely as a result of the Stuart persecution in Scotland, Presbyterianism also got a strong foothold in East Jersey. A shipload of Scots landed in Raritan Bay in 1685 and from there scattered to nearby towns, mostly in Monmouth County. Even though a church was organized

* John E. Pomfret, *The Province of East New Jersey 1609-1702* (Princeton, 1962), 371.
** John E. Pomfret, *The Province of East New Jersey, 1609-1702* (Princeton, 1962), 378.

about 1692 not far from Freehold, the Scottish Presbyterians were unable to secure a settled minister until fourteen years later. Scots, both from Scotland and from Northern Ireland, continued to settle in East Jersey, attracted by the cheap lands and the freedom which the proprietary government promised. Eventually they constituted a very important segment of the population, a fact which was to have considerable bearing on the role played by New Jersey during the Revolutionary War.* Scottish settlements sprang up around Bound Brook on the Raritan and at Baskenridge (Basking Ridge). Still another center of Scottish Presbyterians was at Maidenhead, near the present town of Lawrenceville, just north of Trenton, while individual Scottish families were found in many of the other towns.**

BAPTIST BEGINNINGS

If the provisions regarding religious toleration in East New Jersey proved attractive to Scottish Presbyterians and Congregationalists from New England, they were even more congenial to the Baptists and Quakers. Not only in England, but in most of the American colonies they had been harried and attacked for their peculiar beliefs. It was with relief, then, that they found a haven in New Jersey where freedom of worship was guaranteed by law. Even before the Quaker landings at Salem, there was a Quaker meetinghouse established at Shrewsbury which William Penn visited in 1672. There was also a settlement of Quakers at Middletown along with several Baptist families. Though Baptists are recorded as being in Middletown as early as 1665, they were unable to organize a church until 1688, presumably because they were unable to secure a minister. The following year a church

* George S. Pryde, "The Scots in East New Jersey," *Proceedings of The New Jersey Historical Society*, XV, No. 1, 36, 37. See also Charles A. Briggs, *American Presbyterianism its Origin and Early History* (New York, 1885), 121-123.

** Nelson R. Burr, "The Religious History of New Jersey Before 1702," *Proceedings of The New Jersey Historical Society*, LVI, No. 3, 182ff.

was begun by Baptist families living in Piscataway.* Elsewhere, also, were individual Baptist families though they did not become numerous until later. It was in West New Jersey that the principal Baptist centers were located. At Cohansey in the south a Baptist church was formed by Irish, English, and Welsh immigrants. For a time they were served by ministers from the Baptist colony in Rhode Island.

The man chiefly responsible for gathering the scattered Baptist communions together was Elias Keach, the unordained son of a well-known Baptist preacher in England. Apparently he had learned much from hearing his father, because he appeared before a congregation of Baptists in Pennypack, Pennsylvania, in clerical garb posing as an ordained clergyman. There he began to preach until suddenly he broke down and confessed his imposture to the amazed congregation. His preaching, however, had been so effective that they baptized and ordained him forthwith. Keach proved to be an exceptional preacher and evangelist. Not content with ministering to the scattered Baptists of eastern Pennsylvania, he crossed the Delaware and itinerated widely throughout New Jersey. In company with Thomas Killingsworth, another Baptist missionary, he helped establish Baptist churches wherever he could find a number of Baptist families located. Then he began relating the various congregations to one another in quarterly meetings which greatly strengthened that communion. Keach founded churches and ordained ministers to serve them. Thus Middletown and Piscataway received their first resident pastors and eventually churches were located at Scotch Plains and Morristown.**

A split in the Piscataway Baptist Church was the origin of another small denomination, the Seventh Day Baptists. One of the members, Hezekiah Bonham, was

* Norman Maring, *A History of New Jersey Baptists* (unpublished MS held by New Jersey Baptist Convention, East Orange) Chapter I, 5-6.

** Nelson R. Burr, "The Religious History of New Jersey Before 1702," *Proceedings of The New Jersey Historical Society*, LVI, No. 3, 186, 187. See John E. Pomfret, *The Province of West Jersey, 1609-1702* (Princeton, 1956), 272-276.

taken to task by a church leader named Edmund Dunham for working on Sunday. When Bonham challenged him to prove that the Bible forbade work on the first day of the week, Dunham began a careful study of the relevant passages of Scripture. Not only was he unable to discover any basis for prohibiting Sunday labor, but he became convinced that the Fourth Commandment was still in force for Christians as well as Jews. Accordingly, he and 16 others who were also convinced withdrew from the congregation in 1705 and organized themselves into a separate church, the Seventh Day Baptists. Later on other congregations of Seventh Day Baptists were established at Shiloh and Shrewsbury.*

Still another church body which drew much of its strength from the Baptists was the Universalist Church. It seems to have had its origin in New Jersey when members of the Ephrata Society of eastern Pennsylvania made a preaching tour in 1744 to the Jersey shore near Barnegat Bay. The Ephrata Society, a communistic, celibate order founded by a German Baptist named Conrad Beissel, held the view that all men will ultimately be saved. Among the converts to universal salvation made on this tour was a family named Potter which was Baptist and Quaker in background, and it was Thomas Potter who persuaded the Reverend John Murray, a convert from English Methodism, to become a preacher for the Universalist cause. By 1790 when the first Universalist Convention was held in Philadelphia, there were six New Jersey churches represented. The Baptist pastors of Kingswood, Cape May, and Pittsgrove became Universalist, and by the end of that year four of the fifteen Baptist ministers in the colony had defected to the Universalist cause.**

* *Inventory of the Church Archives of New Jersey: Baptist Bodies* (Newark, 1938), 119-122. See also *Seventh Day Baptist Supplement* (Newark, 1939).

** Clinton L. Scott, *The Universalist Church of America* (Boston, 1957), 8-15. See also Norman H. Maring, *A History of New Jersey Baptists* (Unpublished MS held by New Jersey Baptist Convention, East Orange), Chapter III, 1-5.

Even though the Dutch were the first Europeans to settle in East New Jersey, they were slow in establishing churches. After Bergen was founded, in 1660, as a forti- fied town to protect the Dutch settlers from Indian attack, Governor Peter Stuyvesant sent urgent pleas to the Classis of Amsterdam in the Netherlands requesting

Wood cut of Old Bergen Church, Dutch Reformed
From Barber & Howe,
Historical Collections, 1844

additional ministers. The Classis was the church judica- tory having control over all the Dutch Reformed church members in the colony, and it was responsible for supply- ing ministers for all Dutch enterprises overseas. Unhap- pily, the ministers did not come, but the citizens of Bergen set about organizing a church anyway, the first in New Jersey. Included in its membership were all the Dutch settlers on the west side of the Hudson River until the church at Hackensack was founded some years later. Even though there was no settled minister, there were lay readers to read the liturgy, and a school was established which taught the children the catechism and reading and writing. In 1680 a commodious stone church was erected in place of the first wooden structure, and shortly afterward a Reformed Dutch church was organized at Hackensack. These churches were served by occasional visits from ministers of the Collegiate Dutch Church on Manhattan until Peter Tesschenmaeker, an itinerant Dutch minister, began a circuit of all the Dutch communities west of the Hudson. The wonder is that these churches managed to survive at all, yet they not only survived but flourished, drawn together by the need to perpetuate their Dutch heritage which had such deep religious roots.

One of the Dutch churches of especial interest was located at Aquackanonk on the Passaic River. Its founding was due in large measure to an immigrant named Guiliam Bertholf, a layman, who before coming to America had become associated with an evangelical, pietistic group in western Germany known as the Coelmanists. They were critical of formalism in worship and a religious expression which placed more emphasis on theological orthodoxy than on a warm evangelical life. When Bertholf and his family came to Aquackanonk, he joined the Bergen Church, but served as a layreader and schoolmaster in Hackensack. The Dutch people appreciated his services so much that they sent him to the Netherlands for an education, despite the fact that his pietism had aroused the animosity of the other Dutch pastors in Manhattan. Eventually he was ordained, not by the Classis of Amsterdam which had jurisdiction over the churches in America, but by the Classis of Middleburg. In 1694 he became pastor of the churches at Hackensack and Aquackanonk. There was apparently little love lost between Bertholf and the other Dutch pastors, and communication between them was meager. Bertholf was independent of almost all ecclesiastical control. He does not appear to have communicated with the Classis of Amsterdam or any other classis, for that matter. Yet he was far from parochial in his interests, because he ministered to all the Dutch churches west of the Hudson, visiting them as often as possible. Not only was he the first resident minister of his church in New Jersey, but his evangelical zeal laid an important foundation for the Evangelical Awakening of the eighteenth century.

EARLY ANGLICANISM

Ironically, the weakest of the churches in New Jersey during the seventeenth century was the Anglican, despite the fact that the colony was under the ultimate control of the English crown. There were good reasons for this condition. The very provisions of religious liberty which the proprietors had inserted to encourage immigration, brought to New Jersey refugees from the repressive religious measures of an Anglican monarch. Most of the settlers had good cause to fear the established Church of England and therefore opposed its spread in the colony. At the same time, there was little effort on the part of the Anglican hierarchy to send well qualified priests to establish churches for the colonists. Thus the leadership problem which was common to all the denominations was particularly acute for the Anglicans. Among their number were some of the leading men of East New Jersey, but they were few, and opportunities for them to worship according to the tradition of their faith were fewer still. Most of the time during the proprietary period the only Anglican priest was the chaplain to the royal garrison quartered at the fort on the southern tip of Manhattan Island. By special arrangement with the Dutch Consistory, services in the Anglican rite were celebrated in the Dutch Reformed Church when it was not being used by the Dutch congregation. Whenever Anglicans from the Jersey coast made a trip to New York, which happened fairly frequently, they worshipped with the garrison. At other times the chaplain made a tour of centers such as Perth Amboy and Elizabethtown ministering to the handful of Episcopalians living there.

When the Glorious Revolution of 1688 toppled King James II from his throne, another casualty was the Reverend Alexander Innes who was forced to leave his position as chaplain in Manhattan because of his strong royalist views and his opposition to the revolution. Instead of returning to England, which might not have been very congenial under the circumstances, he took up residence in East Jersey and traveled about seeking those with Anglican sympathies, ministering to them, and paving the way for the organization later on of Anglican churches.

One of the men who took a keen interest in the matter was Colonel Lewis Morris, a wealthy plantation owner near Shrewsbury who was a member of the Governor's Council. He wrote a "Memorial Concerning the State of Religion in the Jerseys, 1700," * which gave a caustic and not unbiased description of the main centers of religious life, particularly in East New Jersey. The inhabitants of Bergen and Aquackanonk were mostly Dutch Calvinists from New York whom he praised for their willingness to support a settled ministery. Elizabethtown, Newark, and Woodbridge were settled mostly by Englishmen of Congregationalist persuasion with a scattering of Presbyterians, Anabaptists, and Quakers among them. Piscataway he called the Anabaptist town. In Freehold, "about one half are Scotch Presbiterians [sic] and the rest have no religion." Middletown had been settled by people from New York and New England for whom "there is no such thing as Church or Religion . . . they are p'haps the most ignorant and wicked People in the world." Of Shrewsbury which contained settlers from New England, Rhode Island, and New York, Morris commented: "There is in it ab't thirty Quakers of both Sexes,

* Found in *Proceedings of The New Jersey Historical Society*, IV, No. 3, 118-121. See comment in *The Biblical Repertory and Princeton Review*, XXIV (1852), 364.

and they have a meeting house, the rest of the People are generally of no religion." * It is evident from the tone of the pamphlet that Colonel Morris laid most of the blame for the religious wasteland in the province upon the rampant sectarianism all about him. The lack of any authoritarian church or religious establishment led, he felt, to loss of interest in religion altogether. Since the pamphlet seems to have originated in a query from Anglican leaders in England regarding the religious state of the Jerseys, we are not surprised to find that Colonel Morris closes with an appeal for the support of the Church in his area. To get worthy priests for the colony he suggested:

Let the King, the A[rch]bishop, ye Bishops and Great Men admit no Man for so many years to any great Benefice, but such as shall oblige themselves to preach three years gratis in America, with part of the living let him maintain a Curate, & the other part let him apply to his own use. By this means we shall have the greatest & best men & in human probability such men must in short time make a wonderful progress in the Conversion of those Countries.**

The plea of Colonel Morris at first did not seem to have much impact. Suspicion of the Anglican establishment was too deeply rooted in the colony to allow any support for his project. The English hierarchy, also, paid slight attention to the proposal, and as a consequence there seemed little promise of success for the Church of England in the two proprietorships of New Jersey. In addition there was not much indication that East and West Jersey would come into closer contact with each other. The two parts of the state were more sharply divided on most issues than Connecticut and New York. The man chiefly responsible for changing both of these

* Found in *Proceedings of The New Jersey Historical Society*, IV, No. 3, 118-121. See comment in *The Biblical Repertory and Princeton Review*, XXIV (1852), 364.
** *Proceedings of The New Jersey Historical Society*, IV, No. 3, 120-121.

conditions was a meteoric individual by the name of George Keith, a Scotsman who began as a Presbyterian, became a Quaker leader, and finally converted to the Anglican Church. His life, which was filled with conflict and recrimination, was to have a profound effect on the rise of Anglicanism in New Jersey, but even more important, it did much to bring the two parts of the state into contact with one another.

As a young man growing up in Scotland Keith had the benefits of an excellent classical education in philosophy, mathematics, and Greek and Latin. He was also well versed in logic which appealed to his orderly mind and gave him an abiding confidence in open debate as a valid way to overcome error and vindicate the truth. Even though he was brought up on the Westminster Catechism and Calvinistic theology, Keith was repelled by the sterile dogmatism of the Scottish Church and the divisive tendency which had shattered the Church into a dozen or more competing sects. It was while serving as a tutor in Edinburgh that he met some Quakers and was quickly drawn to the warm evangelicalism of their fellowship, a warmth that was so notably lacking in his own communion. Eventually he joined the Edinburgh Friends Meeting and quickly became one of its most important members. The Quakers were always under attack in Scotland just as they were in England, and since Keith was already trained for logical controversy he became one of the most prominent apologists for the religion of the "Inner Light." Even more important, perhaps, for the Quaker cause was Keith's ability to write, and from his pen there came a flood of pamphlets and tracts attacking the established churches and vindicating his own. The authorities were quick to take action with the result that Keith was jailed several times, during which periods he usually produced more pamphlets. It was because of his training in mathematics and his ability as a surveyor that he came to the New World.

In 1684 an invitation reached Keith from the Governor of East Jersey, Robert Barclay, who was also a personal friend, to become surveyor-general of the province. It is a commentary on the lack of close contact between the two Jerseys that Keith's first task was to survey the line dividing them, but his real concern was still religious. He debated vigorously with Baptists and Calvinists alike, upholding the Quaker tenets. At the same time, however, he became increasingly concerned about the lack of orthodoxy among his coreligionists. Many Friends showed little concern for theology or even the Bible, relying on the "Inner Light" for their guidance. Keith sensed that this would ultimately lead to chaos with each man becoming his own authority. Aroused by this tendency, Keith began issuing pamphlets which insisted that the "Inner Light" was not enough, but that it must always be under the judgment of Biblical revelation. Soon Keith found himself under attack by several of the meetings in Jersey, and as quickly he attacked them. There was a sizable number of Friends who were convinced by his doctrine, so the conflict implacably led to schism. In 1692 Keith and his followers were expelled from the Quaker fellowship and shortly thereafter they founded the Society of Christian Quakers. This did not satisfy Keith, however. He still believed in the truth of his position and was convinced that the Quakers of Philadelphia and Burlington were too ignorant to see it. So he took ship for London to lay his case before the London Yearly Meeting, the supreme authority for the Society of Friends. The results in London, however, were the same as in Burlington, and Keith and his doctrines were again barred.

With no anchor to windward, Keith drifted for a time. He was seeking for a church-home where both theological order and evangelical zeal could be found, and he discovered it, of all places, in the Church of England! New winds were blowing in that ancient institution which showed in the quite unfamiliar concern for evangelism that many Anglican clergy began to express. Led in large measure by a dynamic missioner named Thomas Bray, the Church began to consider seriously its responsibility for extending the Gospel to the New World. Out of this revived concern came two institutions: the Society for the Promotion of Christian Knowledge, founded in 1699, and the Society for the Propagation of the Gospel in Foreign Parts, in 1701. The latter was the agency to secure and support missionaries, and the former supplied them with libraries and tracts. George Keith, who by now had been received into the Anglican Church and had been ordained a priest, was enlisted as the first missionary to go out with the specific task of traveling through the colonies and suggesting to the Society reasonable courses of action.

On the way over he persuaded the ship's chaplain, the Reverend John Talbot, to join him in his preaching mission. The two of them landed in Boston and conducted services among the known Anglicans in the area, and they engaged in religious controversy with any sectarian leaders who were willing to cross verbal swords. Traveling south they spent seven months in the Middle Colonies. There Keith made a special effort to reach the Quakers and draw them into the Anglican fold. Many of the remaining Christian Quakers did come over, but the main body of the Quakers was unaffected by his appeals. Taking no chances, several of the leading Quaker preachers followed Keith and Talbot to answer the charges which the two Anglicans brought against Quaker doctrine and practice. At the same time, the preaching mission was not without solid results. A number of families who had been Anglican in the old country but had had no opportunity for worship since landing in America now welcomed the chance to worship according to the Book of Common Prayer. When Keith sailed for England in 1704 to become rector of a church in Sussex, he left John Talbot behind to be minister of the newly formed church of St. Mary's at Burlington. Within a few years Anglican churches were formed in Freehold, Shrewsbury, and Middletown. This was quite a change from the complaint of Colonel Morris who claimed that as late as 1700 there were only twelve Anglicans in all East Jersey. There is good reason to believe that this figure was much too low, but the change in the situation of the Anglican communion in the following ten years was dramatic, notwithstanding.

By the time the proprietors surrendered the government of both East and West Jersey to Queen Anne in 1702 the Quaker hegemony of West Jersey had already been broken and the two parts of the state had been brought into much closer contact with each other. John Talbot, in a letter to the Secretary of the Society for the Propagation of the Gospel on April 7, 1704, gave much of the credit for this achievement to George Keith:

I may say, he has done more for the Church than any, yea, than all before him. He came worthy of his mission and the Gospel of Christ. Taking nothing of the heathen he came to proselyze [sic]; besides his ordinary or rather extraordinary travels, his preaching excellent sermons upon all occasions, his disputes with all sorts of Heathen and Hereticks (who superabound in these parts—Africa hath not more monsters than America.)*

While the Presbyterians, Baptists, and most certainly the Quakers would take exception to the remarks of Mr. Talbot, there is no denying that George Keith did contribute to one characteristic of religion in New Jersey which was to become even more marked in the future: the wide diversity of its church organizations competing with one another and yet learning to get along with one another in a sort of tolerant partnership.

* Quoted by C. S. Lewis, "George Keith, the Missionary," *Proceedings of The New Jersey Historical Society*, XIII, No. 1, 38-45.

II

DIVERSITY TAKES ROOT
1702-1776

THE DUTCH SETTLERS of New York and New Jersey at the beginning of the eighteenth century were a stolid lot renowned for their industry and orthodoxy. They prized above all their close ties with the Mother Country, the Netherlands, and insisted that the Gospel reached its perfection only when proclaimed in pure Dutch. For this reason, the first pastors of the Dutch Reformed Church in New Jersey were all a bit suspected by their fellows in New York. Peter Tesschenmaeker had been ordained by a self-proclaimed classis of American clergy without prior approval of the Classis of Amsterdam. Guiliam Bertholf, even though educated and ordained in Holland, did not accept the jurisdiction of the Amsterdam Classis, and furthermore, he had absorbed some of the German pietism of his early associations before coming to this country. The most controversial by far, however, of these early Dutch dominies, was Theodorus Jacobus Frelinghuysen, a vigorous preacher and fearless proponent of an independent American church.

No one ever accused Frelinghuysen of too much caution or too much tact. He was a man with strong viewpoints on every issue, and many of his ideas clashed with those prevalent in the colony. Unlike most of the Dutch Reformed membership, Frelinghuysen had been born in Westphalia, Germany, and had had a good education for his day. He joined the Dutch Reformed Church because it had a strong reputation for orthodoxy, and after ordination he served a pastorate near Emden. What led him to leave the Netherlands and travel to the New World is not known. Perhaps it was impatience with the formalism and superficiality of religion as he found it in the Netherlands. While in the Netherlands, Frelinghuysen had been greatly influenced by the evangelical minority within the Dutch church. Somewhat like the German pietists across the border, they advocated a personal approach to religion with emphasis upon individual conversion and an experience of God in Christ. Unlike the pietists, however, Frelinghuysen adhered strictly to the creeds and standards of the Church, especially the Heidelberg Catechism. In theology he was completely orthodox. Only in an insistence on Christian practice did he differ from many of his colleagues.*

Whatever the reason, Frelinghuysen accepted a call from the Dutch church at Raritan and arrived in New York during January of 1720. The pastor of the Collegiate Church there, the Reverend Henricus Boel, invited him as a courtesy to preach, though no doubt he was curious to see what sort of man the new dominie would turn out to be. He soon found out. During the worship service, Frelinghuysen refused to be bound to the forms of the church, omitted the Lord's Prayer since he felt recitation of it was merely rote, and then he accused Dominie Du Bois of extravagance for having a large looking glass in the house.**

A few days later Frelinghuysen reached Raritan and began preaching to his new congregation. Apparently he began with the idea that most Dutch congregations were unregenerate and so all, including members of the Church, needed a conversion experience. This was not exactly what the solid Dutch farmers of his congregation

* See Leonard J. Trinterud, *The Forming of an American Tradition* (Philadelphia, 1949), 54-56.
** *Ecclesiastical Records of the State of New York* (Albany, 1916), 2259-2260.

were expecting in their new dominie. They had organized their church largely without benefit of clergy, and they clung tenaciously to the forms of religion inherited from their homeland. Now to be told from the pulpit that

the nominal and formal Christian [who] contents himself with the external performance, however diligent in the observance of the institutions of religion, God regards as an idolater *

was a shock, to say the least. Frelinghuysen was not long in asserting that many of his most important parishioners were, in his estimation, to be classified as "nominal and formal." Such forthright accusations were bound to create trouble, and they did. A number of leading members of the congregation appealed to the Dutch ministers of New York against what they said were Frelinghuysen's unorthodox views. In response Frelinghuysen published three of his sermons to support his orthodoxy and then proceeded to excommunicate four of the outraged members when they refused to appear before the Raritan Consistory. Determined to effect a thoroughgoing reformation in the Raritan and Three-Mile Run churches, Frelinghuysen insisted on the right to nominate all candidates for the offices of elder and deacon in these congregations.** Such autocratic behavior was insupportable to many of the church members who had managed to run their church for many years with no pastor at all. The dissidents assembled their charges in a "Complaint Against Frelinghuysen" † which was supported by the signatures of 64 members of four Dutch churches in the Raritan area. Four New York dominies, including Boel and Du Bois, supported the "Complaint." At the same

* T. J. Frelinghuysen, *Sermons* (New York, 1856), 26.
** *Ecclesiastical Records of the State of New York* (Albany, 1916), 2249.
† For a full account of the "Complaint" and the correspondence relating to it, see *Ecclesiastical Records of the State of New York* (Albany, 1916), IV *passim*.

time there were a number of Dutch pastors, especially Bertholf of Hackensack and Freeman of Long Island, who came to Frelinghuysen's aid. Furthermore, once the initial shock wore off, a substantial majority of Frelinghuysen's flock accepted both his leadership and his doctrine.

The issue, of course, was not purely doctrinal. Some of it was a question of personalities, but most of all it was a difference regarding the nature of the Christian life. Without realizing it, many of the Dutch settlers made of their religion a means of defending their national heritage. Thus it consisted primarily in the preservation of the Dutch Reformed creeds as expressed in the Dutch language. Frelinghuysen challenged this view. Influenced by Dutch evangelicalism, he insisted that the prime function of religion is the transformation of life by relating each individual believer directly to God through a conversion experience. As it turned out, time was on Frelinghuysen's side. His evangelical preaching began to permeate the raw frontier life of early eighteenth-century New Jersey in a way the staid orthodoxy of the older Dutch churches could never have done. Even more important, however, the emphasis of Frelinghuysen made it possible for the Dutch churches to relate themselves in a positive way to non-Dutch communities in New Jersey. In other words, whereas the older orthodoxy was more a defense mechanism to protect the Dutch culture from outside encroachment, the new evangelicalism of Frelinghuysen began to reach out to kindred souls of whatever national background and reform them in the name of the Gospel.* The far-reaching effects of Frelinghuysen's ministry did not become fully apparent until

* Three of the men whom Frelinghuysen excommunicated attacked him in a letter for associating in a worship service with a Presbyterian: "You did permit a dissenting candidate, in one of the churches where you preached, at the Communion, to offer a prayer in English, before a Dutch congregation. . . . Is there to be no accounting for this before Divine and Ecclesiastical judgment seats?" *Ecclesiastical Records of the State of New York* (Albany, 1916), 2466.

George Whitefield's visits to America launched the Great Awakening. But the ground was prepared for his coming by the preaching of the Dutch pastor on the Raritan.

Out of the dispute over Frelinghuysen's orthodoxy, which dragged on for nearly eight years, came the conviction that the Dutch Reformed Church needed an American judicatory to handle church disputes of a local nature. Frelinghuysen, naturally, was a strong supporter of the plan. He not only supported the "Coetus," as the new judicatory was called, but an American college to train candidates for pastorates in the Reformed Church, especially after he lost two of his sons at sea on their way back from receiving a theological education in the Netherlands.* Again, it was the New York ministers who were the chief opponents of the coetus so that it was not until 1747 that such an organization was formed and, a few years later, led to a split in the Church. Ultimately, of course, the men who stubbornly sought to "keep things in the Dutch way, in our churches." ** had to give way to a more ecumenical approach, but the dispute was not finally settled until just before the Revolutionary War.

PRESBYTERIAN PROGRESS

The other Calvinistic group that played an important part in the religious life of New Jersey during this period was the Presbyterian. Even though the earliest English Calvinists in East Jersey were of Puritan stock from New England, most of them were quietly absorbed into the Presbyterian Church by the time of the Revolution. The Congregational Church at Woodbridge became Presbyterian as early as 1710. The Puritan congregation at Elizabethtown followed suit in 1717, and even the con-

* *Manual of the Reformed Church in America* (4th ed.; New York, 1902), 106.
** *Ecclesiastical Records of the State of New York* (Albany, 1916), 2587.

gregation at Newark entered the Presbyterian fold.*
There were several good reasons for this development,
so much so that the union was accomplished with scarcely
a murmur of dissent. It had been the hope of the first
Puritan settlers that by moving to the freer environment
of New Jersey they would not only be able to recover
a stricter practice of church membership but would also
escape the encroachments of the English Crown, which
was whittling away at the traditional freedoms of the
New England colonies. After 1702, however, the Crown
took over control of New Jersey as well, so that the
Congregational churches were faced with the same encroachments on their liberties which had already been
the lot of their religious brothers to the north. In this
situation, some form of united stand seemed highly advisable, and the polity of the Presbyterian church lent
itself to that sort of united stand. Furthermore, the Presbyterians and Congregationalists shared exactly the same
credal standards, making union that much easier.

The Presbyterian Church was strengthened, meanwhile, by the emigration from Scotland and northern Ireland of large numbers of Scottish settlers, almost all of
whom were ardent Presbyterians. They were a fighting lot
who remembered the persecutions of their homeland and
bristled at the very word Anglican. The Anglican governor in New York soon made it clear that he planned to
drive out dissenters from both New York and New Jersey
and in their place establish the Anglican Church. The
main reason he failed in the attempt was the opposition
of the Presbyterian Church led by a vigorous Scotch-Irish
minister named Francis Makemie. Coming to America
with two other Presbyterian ministers, Makemie joined
with four ministers already there to constitute a presbytery in Philadelphia in 1706. A short time afterward the

* *Inventory of Church Archives of New Jersey: Congregational
Christian Churches* (Newark, 1941), 6. See W. S. Nichols, "Early
Newark as a Puritan Theocracy in Colonial New Jersey," *Proceed-
ings of The New Jersey Historical Society,* V, No. 4, 201 ff.

presbytery met in Freehold, New Jersey to ordain John Boyd, the first of a long line of indigenous ministers. Later Makemie preached at Woodbridge and then moved to New York where he was invited to preach in a private home by local Presbyterians. It was shortly after this that Makemie was arrested by order of Edward, Lord Cornbury, Governor of New York and New Jersey, for preaching without a license. The case did not come to court until June of 1707 at which time Makemie was defended by three able New York attorneys, basing their defense on the fact that Makemie had a license to preach as a dissenting minister which had been issued in Barbados and recognized in Virginia and, therefore, was presumably valid in any British territory or colony. The court finally found in favor of the defendant, but Lord Cornbury was so incensed that he ordered Makemie to pay the entire court costs, a sum roughly equivalent to one year's salary. It was this final act that led the New York Asembly to pass a law making it illegal to assess an acquitted prisoner with his court costs. They also directed a complaint to the Crown which led to Cornbury's recall to England.*

Even though Makemie died the year following his trial, his fearless defense and his victory over the tyranny of Lord Cornbury added immensely to the prestige of the Presbyterians as the champions of freedom. It also brought its problems. The growth of the Presbyterian Church in New Jersey, the addition of the Puritan Congregationalists to the Presbyterian fold, and the rather haphazard control of presbytery led to a considerable diversity within the church. By 1716 the Presbytery of Philadelphia divided into three subordinate presbyteries which together were to form the Synod of Philadelphia.

---

* The court transcript of the proceedings is recorded in Makemie's pamphlet, "A Narrative of a New and Unusual American Imprisonment of two Presbyterian Ministers . . . by a Learner of Law and Lover of Liberty" (Boston, 1707). See L. P. Bowen, *The Days of Makemie, or, the Vine Planted* (Philadelphia, 1885), Chapters 28 and 29.

The churches of New Jersey continued in the reconstituted presbytery of Philadelphia while new presbyteries were formed for the churches in Maryland, Delaware, and Pennsylvania and in Long Island. To the conservative Presbyterian pastors of Philadelphia and Delaware the diversity within the church was looked upon as a serious threat. In 1721 minister from that area sought to make subscription to the Westminster Confession and Catechisms obligatory for all Presbyterian ministers. This launched a vigorous debate in which the Scotch-Irish Presbyterians of the south were ranged against the more liberal English Presbyterian ministers of the north.

By all odds the most able and effective leader in the subscription controversy was Jonathan Dickinson, pastor of the church in Elizabethtown. It was largely due to his conciliatory spirit that a schism was avoided, and the Synod passed the famous Adopting Act in 1729 which was to have the most profound effect on the subsequent history of the denomination. The Adopting Act was a shrewd compromise. It established the rule that all Presbyterian ministers must declare their agreement with the Westminster Standards "as being in all the essential and necessary articles, good forms of sound words and systems of Christian doctrine." It further provided that in case of question the presbyteries or synod would determine what were the "essential and necessary articles." * Yet even this was not enough, because the conservatives continued to press for more strict controls while the liberals insisted on a freer interpretation of the Standards.

In 1738 New Jersey was divided into two presbyteries. The northern part of the state became part of the Presbytery of New York, and the central Jersey churches were organized into the Presbytery of New Brunswick. Many of the ministers in New Brunswick Presbytery were products of a remarkable institution known as the "Log College," a private theological school operated by the Reverend William Tennent, Sr., at Neshaminy, Pennsyl-

* Quoted in Charles A. Briggs, *American Presbyterianism* (New York, 1885), 218ff.

vania, just north of Philadelphia. Like the Dutch Reformed, the Presbyterians were hampered in their expansion by the difficulty of securing a trained ministry. The chief source of supply, up to this time, was either the British Isles or New England, both of which were too far away to attract many candidates. So the Log College filled a real need. Opposition to the Log College men, however, built up in Philadelphia. It was not really the scholarship of these candidates that was in question but rather their evangelistic zeal. William Tennent trained his sons to be evangelists as well as pastors, and their concern for conversion and for spiritual lives rather than doctrinal orthodoxy led to an attempt by the Philadelphia ministers to exclude the Log College men from the Presbyterian ministry.

REVIVAL IN NEW JERSEY

What brought the matter to a head was the revival in the Middle Colonies known as the "Great Awakening." In New Brunswick, Gilbert Tennent, the son of William Tennent, Sr., who was pastor of the Presbyterian Church began to preach evangelistic sermons aimed at the radical conversion of his congregation. He became a close friend of Frelinghuysen, and the two began exchanging pulpits and itinerating in the surrounding area. In 1738 the revival was greatly accelerated by the visit of George Whitefield, one of the most magnetic preachers of all time. His powerful voice and urgent messages stirred people wherever he went, and they flocked by the thousands to hear him. Even Benjamin Franklin, whose views on religion were anything but emotional, was impressed by the English evangelist. Gilbert Tennent and the other Log College men welcomed Whitefield when he visited New Jersey in 1739 and associated themselves with his ministry, even though he was still an Anglican at that time. The combination of evangelistic zeal and cooperation with non-Presbyterians made the Awakening suspect to the Philadelphia clergy, and they proceeded to get the Synod to pass a rule that any candidate for the ministry

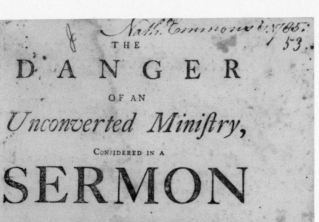

THE

DANGER

OF AN

Unconverted Ministry,

CONSIDERED IN A

SERMON

On MARK VI. 34.

By *Gilbert Tennent*, A. M.

And Minister of the Gospel in *New-Brunswick, New-Jersey.*

JEREM. V. 30, 31. *A wonderful and horrible Thing is committed in the Land: The Prophets prophesy falsely, and the Priests bear Rule by their Means, and my People love to have it so; and what will they do in the End thereof?*

From the Second Edition printed at *Philadelphia.*

BOSTON, Printed and Sold by *Rogers* and *Fowle* below the Prison in Queen-Street, near the TOWN-HOUSE. 1742.

Facsimile title page of Gilbert Tennent's sermon, "The Danger of an Unconverted Ministry," 1742

who did not have a diploma from a European or New England college would have to be examined by the Synod. Thus the Log College was refused recognition as a valid school of the ministry and the traditional right of the presbytery to examine candidates for the ministry was taken over by the larger judicatory, the Synod.

Obviously, the New Brunswick Presbytery was not

going to permit such an action to go unchallenged. Ignoring the act of the Synod, the New Brunswick Presbytery licensed John Rowland to preach, even though he was a Log College man. The Synod, which was controlled by the anti-revival faction, declared the licensing illegal and reprimanded the Presbytery. Thus the Log College party was soundly defeated, and its opponents had grounds for believing that it might be stamped out entirely. What changed the balance of power was the progress of the revival movement in the Middle Colonies under the impassioned preaching of George Whitefield, William Tennent, Sr., and his three sons, as well as Frelinghuysen and other men like him. The lay members of the church heard these men and liked what they heard. Instead of theological hair-splitting with little personal relevance, the revivalists spoke to the needs of common people in a language they could understand. Whenever a church became vacant, the congregation asked first of all for a Log College man. Gilbert Tennent attacked the anti-revivalists at their weakest point in his sermon, "The Danger of an Unconverted Ministry":

Look into the Congregations of unconverted Ministers, and see what a sad Security reigns there; not a Soul convinced that can be heard of, for many Years together; and yet the Ministers are easy; for they say they do their Duty! . . . But let such hireling murderous Hypocrites take Care, that they don't feel the Force of a Halter in this World, and an aggravated Damnation in the next.*

The words stung, particularly since charges of drunkenness, plagiarism, and sexual immorality were frequently brought against ministers in the anti-revival camp. It was evident that the two parties were no longer able to remain in one church, so after the Synod meeting of 1741, the majority, called the Old Side, ejected the Log College Men and the New Brunswick Presbytery. This latter

* Quoted in Armstrong, Loetscher, and Anderson, *The Presbyterian Enterprise* (Philadelphia, 1956), 42.

group, the New Side, reorganized as the Synod of New York in 1745 embracing the presbyteries of New Brunswick, New York and Londonderry in New Hampshire.

The Log College which had been the center of the dispute came to an end about this time when William Tennent, Sr. resigned his pastorate and sold his property including the two-story log building where the students had been housed and taught. This, of course, confronted the New Side Synod with the problem of training additional men for the ministry. As long as the Log College was in operation, the New Brunswick Presbytery had an enviable advantage over the conservatives of Philadelphia, since the Log College produced more ministerial candidates than came from Britain or New England. It therefore became imperative to secure another college. Unfortunately, every college had to be chartered by the State, and Governor Lewis Morris, a strong Anglican, refused to charter a Presbyterian school. As soon as he died, however, four ministers in New York Presbytery secured a charter from the interim governor in 1746 to create the College of New Jersey. For six months it met in the home of its founder and first president, Jonathan Dickinson, at Elizabethtown. It was then moved to Newark to the parsonage of its second president, the Reverend Aaron Burr. In 1748 Jonathan Belcher became Governor of New Jersey and at once took a deep and lasting interest in the college. He granted it a permanent charter and was instrumental in giving it a permanent location at Princeton in 1754.*

From then on Princeton College provided an increasing number of ministers for the New Side churches of New Jersey and New York. In addition, recruits were secured from the New England colleges which had also come under the influence of the Great Awakening. By contrast, the Old Side Synod remained virtually static in the number of its ministers and its churches. One of the New England ministers whose lonely life made him

* Cf. Nelson R. Burr, *Education in New Jersey 1630-1871* (Princeton, 1942), Chapter IX.

almost a legend was David Brainerd. As a student in Yale College he had heard Gilbert Tennent preach while on a preaching mission in New England and had been moved by the revivalism of Jonathan Edwards and James Davenport. The College authorities were largely against the revival, however, so when Brainerd criticized one of the tutors as having "no·more grace than this chair" he was summarily ejected from the school.* After studying privately with an evangelical Congregational minister, he was engaged by the Scottish Society for Propagating Christian Knowledge to conduct a mission to the Indians. In 1744 he was ordained at Newark by the Presbytery of New York and then began work among the Indians along the Delaware. At Crossweeksung, the modern Crosswicks, Brainerd had his greatest success in a settlement of the Lenni Lenape Indians. Even while his body was ravaged by tuberculosis he organized a congregation of converts, began a school, and taught the Indians useful trades, before his early death at the age of thirty. Although his accomplishments in terms of conversions were not impressive, the Journal he kept which was later published by Jonathan Edwards had a profound effect on the foreign missionary movement of the nineteenth century.

Meanwhile Scotch-Irish settlers, almost all of whom were Presbyterians, continued to pour into America. Between 1731 and 1768 about one-third of the Scotch-Irish Presbyterians living in North Ireland sailed to the New World, and many of them settled in New Jersey. By 1765 the Presbyterian churches accounted for one-third of the total number of churches in the colony.** Nearly all of the new churches were organized by the "New Side" Synod of New York which was able to supply ministerial leadership from its own College of New Jersey as well as from Yale College. Perhaps even more important, by

* Jonathan Edwards, *Memoirs of the Rev. David Brainerd* (New Haven, 1822), 52 f. See David Wynbeek, *David Brainerd: Beloved Yankee* (Grand Rapids, 1961).

** Nelson R. Burr, *The Anglican Church in New Jersey* (Philadelphia, 1954), 66.

cooperating with the Great Awakening, the "New Side" churches benefitted from the spiritual revival and provided a spiritual home to those who were converted by the revivalistic preaching. The "Old Side" churches, by their opposition to revival, remained almost static. In 1758 the unfortunate schism which had disrupted the Presbyterian Church was finally healed with the formation of the united Synod of New York and Philadelphia. There was little doubt, however, which group was to have the predominant voice from then on. While the "Old Side" had increased by only four ministers during the schism, the "New Side" had grown by fifty-two.*

ANGLICANS SEEK AN ESTABLISHMENT

It is remarkable that while the Presbyterians were growing so rapidly the Anglican Church in New Jersey made only hesitant advances. Considering the fact that the colony was under the direct authority of the British Crown and that church and state were closely united in Britain, one might have expected a more determined effort to introduce an Anglican establishment overseas. The fact that such an establishment never was created was due as much to apathy in England as to opposition in the Colony. It is true that for a majority of the citizens of New Jersey Anglicanism was a hated word. Many of them had fled England because of religious oppression, and they had no desire to see a similar regime set up on American soil. Furthermore, the lack of Anglican priests in the Colony left those colonists who had a strong attachment to the Church of England without any leadership. Consequently, religious interest waned and the few Anglicans there either joined a dissenting church or lost all religious connection. The chief responsibility for these conditions, of course, must rest with the Anglican hierarchy. Even after Charles I gave jurisdiction over the American parishes to the Bishop of London in 1633,

* Charles A. Briggs, *American Presbyterianism* (New York, 1885), 315.

almost nothing was done to secure an adequate supply of priests for the colonies. The first Anglican priest to labor in New Jersey, the Reverend Alexander Innes, recognized almost no episcopal control after he fled New York, yet he gathered small congregations in Freehold, Shrewsbury, and Middletown before his death in 1713.*

For two years at the end of the seventeenth century East Jersey had a regularly assigned priest in the person of the Reverend Edward Portlock, who was sent overseas by the Bishop of London immediately after his ordination. He seems to have regarded himself more as a chaplain to the Royal Governor than as rector of a church, for he accompanied the Governor on most of his trips through the colony. Portlock was an eccentric sort who was remembered for his attachment to a tabby cat named Alice. When in a fit of jealousy his wife hung the poor creature, Portlock preached a vigorous sermon in church against women in general and his wife in particular.**

It was not until the Society for the Propagation of the Gospel in Foreign Parts sent over Keith and Talbot that much interest was generated in the Anglican Church of the colonies. Talbot, as has been noted, founded the first Episcopal Church in New Jersey, St. Mary's in Burlington. It was the first to have a settled pastor and to have a parish organization. Talbot served the church from 1704 to the time of his death in 1727, even though he was dismissed by the Society on charges of having exceeded his authority and of being sympathetic with the exiled Stuart Pretender to the English throne.

The report of Keith to the Society for the Propagation of the Gospel upon his return to England and the urgent letters of John Talbot led to the sending out of other priests. John Brooke organized an Anglican Church in Elizabethtown for two years, and, after his death, was succeeded by Edward Vaughan who itinerated from

* Nelson R. Burr, *The Anglican Church in New Jersey* (Philadelphia, 1954), 13 f.
** Nelson R. Burr, *The Anglican Church in New Jersey* (Philadelphia, 1954), 636.

Newark to Perth Amboy serving Anglican groups wherever he could find them. Though unspectacular, growth was consistent, and by 1740 there were six missionary priests laboring in New Jersey under the support of the Society for the Propagation of the Gospel. The most serious drawback to continued growth was the difficulty of securing additional ministerial candidates. Reports to the Society are full of appeals not only for additional clergy but for a bishop who could train and ordain men on the scene. The English hierarchy, however, were in no mood to accede to these requests. Already the colonies were noted for their independent ways, and most Englishmen, at least those in the government, felt that the colonists should be brought under stricter control. If the Anglicans were to secure a bishop in New Jersey, was the reasoning, they could throw off all church ties with England. For different reasons, the Dissenters in England and the non-Anglican majority in the Colony were just as strong in their opposition to the establishment of a bishop in New Jersey. Thus each request for a bishop was either ignored or denied.

How long the even growth of the Anglican church would have continued, we cannot know, because during the 1740's it became embroiled in the tide of the Great Awakening. We have seen how this tide contributed to a schism in the Presbyterian Church. Indeed there was no denomination which was unaffected by it. In the Middle Colonies it was precipitated by the preaching tour of George Whitefield, even though the Tennents and Frelinghuysen had laid the foundation. Since Whitefield and the Wesleyan preachers associated with him were technically members of the Anglican Church, the Anglicans of New Jersey were immediately involved. At first the Anglican clergy welcomed him to their homes and pulpits. It was almost impossible not to be fascinated by the man, and when he began to preach his deep resonant voice, his vivid and picturesque language, and, above all, the emotional appeal of his message, created converts by the hundreds wherever he went. Between 1739 and 1770

Whitefield visited New Jersey no less than five times, and each time the crowds thronged to hear him. But the missionary priests of the Anglican communion rapidly lost their appreciation for his gifts. For one thing, Whitefield had very little concern for denominational proprieties in an age when denominational distinctions were strong. It mattered little to him whether he preached in an Anglican or a Presbyterian or a Baptist church. He even preached in the open air where more could hear him at one time. In addition, he omitted the use of the Book of Common Prayer whenever he felt that it did not contribute to the need of the hour. For him, the sermon calling the wicked to repentance was the heart of the matter, so the other elements in worship were often disregarded. The fact that to the many unchurched who listened to him this approach made sense, was not regarded by the Anglican traditionalists as sufficient excuse for his unorthodox behavior. But most of all the unabashed appeal to emotionalism angered the English rectors. Nor did it help matters any when Whitefield attacked the coldness and unchristian behavior of the Anglican clergy in his sermons.

In the end Whitefield divided the Anglicans, though it should be noted that this did not produce a schism in the church as it did among the Presbyterians. As the great revivalist moved back and forth across the colony he was welcomed by the "New Side" Presbyterians, the Baptists and many of the German and Dutch settlers, but he was opposed by most of the Anglicans, the "Old Side" Presbyterians, the Quakers, and the rationalists.* Yet even those who opposed him benefitted by his ministry. Those who were offended by the emotional outbursts of the revivalists joined the Anglican Church, and this included a considerable number who previously had had no church connection whatever. The number of Anglicans, on the other hand, who left their church on account of the revivals ultimately proved to be small, and most of them

* Nelson R. Burr, *The Anglican Church in New Jersey* (Philadelphia, 1954), 75.

finally joined a Methodist society somewhere nearby. By this time Whitefield had broken with the Wesley brothers over the matter of predestination and free will, but the Whitefield preaching missions were in great measure responsible for the success of the Methodist movement in New Jersey later on.

METHODISM BEGINS ITS MISSION

It is not clear when the first Methodists came to New Jersey. Since the colony was a thoroughfare for traffic between New York and Philadelphia it is certain that Methodist preachers passed through as soon as Methodist societies were organized in these two large cities, which was around 1769. Richard Boardman, a Methodist preacher on his way to New York conducted services in a town with a British garrison, probably Trenton, in November of that year. The next year Captain Thomas Webb, a British officer, organized a Methodist class in Burlington, and about the same time Joseph Toy organized another class at Trenton. The man, however, who is chiefly responsible for the vigorous growth of Methodism in New Jersey is Francis Asbury, who was sent over to America by John Wesley in 1771. A measure of his dynamic ministry is seen in the fact that when he arrived there were probably not more than thirty or forty Methodists in all the Colony. Less than two years later there were two hundred. Scarcely a town of any size in New Jersey was overlooked by him as he rode ceaselessly from place to place on his preaching mission. While he was an effective preacher and evangelist, his gifts were even more outstanding as an organizer. Wherever he made new converts, he brought them together into a class and taught them how to meet together for continued growth in grace. Unlike the Anglican clergy, the Methodist preachers spoke anywhere they could find an audience, which was usually outside a church building. Two favorite spots were the steps of the local courthouse or jail.* Furthermore, they preached throughout the week and not just on Sunday. This meant that the Methodist preachers were able to reach far more people and meet them more frequently than the ministers who restricted themselves to stated times and seasons for worship. The Methodists also took full advantage of another condition in their favor: the availability of leaders. Unlike the Anglicans they did not need ordination by a bishop in England to permit them to preach, and unlike the Presbyterians they did not require a university education for their preachers. Thus they were able to secure new preachers much more rapidly than most of the other religious bodies could do. William Watters, a native American, was appointed preacher in New Jersey less than two years after Asbury landed. Most important of all for Methodist success was the class system of organization which required no specially trained leadership. Meeting in private homes and led by devout laymen with the periodic assistance of a traveling preacher, the classes provided a means for rapid expansion. The expansion was not long in coming. Up to the Revolutionary War the number of members, the number of circuits, and the list of preachers increased notably each year, thanks to the inspired leadership of Francis Asbury.

The growth, however, came more in the southern part of the state than in the north. Wherever the Methodists encountered a strongly entrenched Presbyterian Church or any church of Calvinist theology the Methodist growth wavered. Only in the south which was sparsely churched and where the predominant religion was Quaker did Methodism flourish. That is not to say that all southern Jerseymen suddenly became Methodists. Even though the traveling preachers of Wesley were amazingly successful in their evangelistic efforts, their fellow Methodists were still only a small minority of the population.

* See Francis Asbury, *Journal*, entries for Mar. 27, Apr. 15, Apr. 30, May 7, and May 29, 1772 (London, 1958).

By far the largest single religious group in south Jersey was still the Society of Friends. In the middle of the eighteenth century, however, they were different from the Friends of a century earlier. Careful management and sober industry had made them prosperous and comfortable. The stories of persecution which their forebears had endured were for them little more than stories. Yet it would not be fair to say that they had declined in zeal. The defection of George Keith had shaken them, but instead of destroying the Society it had merely strengthened its inner discipline. The Quakers were still very much people of discipline and people of conviction. It was from this background of silent worship and mystical experience that John Woolman came, one of the best examples of Quaker life and witness. The Woolman family were plantation owners in the Rancocas Valley, southeast of Burlington. Though John did not have an extensive education, he read a great deal and developed a writing style that was the envy of literary men as far away as England. He learned the tailor's trade and opened a business in Mount Holly which prospered almost from the first, but this did not satisfy the deepest cravings of this sensitive man. When he was twenty-two years old, he had been obliged to make up a bill of sale for a young Negress slave. The number of slaves in New Jersey at this time was fairly large considering the total population. Eleven hundred were owned by Quakers in one Quarterly Meeting alone,* no doubt because of the need of servants and the rising standard of wealth in the Society of Friends. To Woolman, however, the whole idea of human slavery was not only repugnant but impossible to reconcile with a Christian profession. He shared his concern with his fellow Quakers and finally gave up his business and devoted the rest of his life to opposing the traffic in slaves. In this he showed another

* Rufus M. Jones, *The Quakers in the American Colonies* (London, 1911), 395.

Facsimile page of Woolman's *Journal* for April 20, 1767
Rutgers University Library

characteristic dear to the Quaker conscience: the pursuit of simplicity in living. In his Journal he confided:

Through the mercies of the Almighty, I had, in a good degree, learned to be content with a plain way of living. I had but a small family; and, on serious consideration, believed truth did not require me to engage much in cumbering affairs.*

Leaving his wife and daughter in 1757 he traveled on horseback to the various Quaker settlements throughout Virginia. It was the second time that he had been there, and this time his mission was to oppose the ownership of slaves. He did it in a quite unique manner, one far removed from the ferocity of a John Brown or the vituperation of a William Lloyd Garrison. Whenever he came to a Quaker home he showed the letter of introduction from his own Quarterly Meeting. This insured him hospitality, though in Virginia, a land noted for its lavish hospitality, this was usually unnecessary. But if the Quaker with whom he lodged was an owner of slaves, then before he left Woolman insisted on paying in cash for his meals and lodging stating that he refused to accept free hospitality procured from slave labor. It was a touchy business and often caused offense, but so delicately was it done and so sweet was the spirit of the wandering Quaker that in most cases the host took the silver with open-mouthed astonishment. Like David Brainerd, John Woolman's accomplishments at first seemed few. He did not shake the world or make much of a ripple in New Jersey society. But his quiet witness began to crystallize the thoughts of men, especially among the New Jersey Friends so that by 1800 there were very few any longer who retained ownership of slaves. Not content with stirring up the conscience of American Friends regarding slavery, Woolman took ship for London to speak to the Friends there, because London was the thriving center of the slave trade between Africa and the New World. It was a costly trip, since at York, England, Woolman died of smallpox, the same dread disease that had killed his mother years before. Later, when America was locked in mortal combat over the issue of slavery, men would remember both the words and witness of the gentle New Jersey Quaker, John Woolman.

* John Woolman, *Journal* (Boston, 1871), 91.

The Baptist churches of New Jersey grew slowly in number and communicant membership up to the time of the Revolution. They were affected, like all other church bodies, by the Great Awakening, but the revival of religious interest brought about less expansion than one might have expected. The churches at Hopewell and Piscataway continued to flourish, and from the latter daughter congregations were organized at Scotch Plains and Morristown. One reason for the failure of the New Jersey Baptist churches to grow as rapidly as the Baptist churches of the South lay in the fact that most of the former were Regular Baptists with little taste for revivalism. The Separate Baptists who participated actively in the Great Awakening were centered in New England and the South, so that the revival fires which burned so brightly among the Baptists of New England and the Carolinas, scarcely touched the Middle Colonies. As a matter of fact, the New Jersey Baptists differed but little from the Old Light Presbyterians, except in the matter of polity and the sacraments. This was another reason for slow Baptist growth. The two denominations were bitter rivals and wherever the Presbyterians were strong, which was nearly everywhere in the Colony, the Baptists were squeezed out. Illustrative of the feeling between the two church groups was the debate between Abel Morgan, the Baptist minister at Middletown, and Samuel Finley, the Presbyterian who later became president of Princeton College. The two men took part in a vigorous debate at Cape May in 1747, which resulted in a draw. Later Finley wrote a booklet embodying his views on infant baptism entitled, "A Charitable Plea for the Speechless" to which Morgan replied with "Anti-Paedo Rantism: or, Mr. Samuel Finley's Charitable Plea for the Speechless Examined and Refuted."

* Norman Maring, *A History of New Jersey Baptists* (Unpublished MS held by New Jersey Baptist Convention, East Orange), Chapter II, 5 f and 21 f. See Jesse L. Boyd, *A History of Baptists in America Prior to 1845* (New York, 1957), 64.

The most important event during this period was the formation in 1707 of the Philadelphia Association which brought together most of the Baptist churches in New Jersey, eastern Pennsylvania, and southern New York. Until 1751 it was the only continuing Baptist Association in the New World and it soon proved to be invaluable in strengthening the common witness of Baptists throughout the Middle Colonies. The Association fulfilled a number of useful functions from the time of its founding. Even though it did not have jurisdictional control over its member churches as a Presbyterian Synod has, it was a valuable court for the airing of inter-church disputes and for doing those things which a single congregation alone would find impossible. Among these was the founding of Rhode Island College, later Brown University. Despite the doubts of some Baptists regarding the scriptural basis for an educated ministry, the Association helped raise funds for the new college which was finally chartered in 1764. When Isaac Eaton, pastor of the Baptist Church of Hopewell, began a grammar school in 1756, the Association gave its encouragement and support. The Hopewell Academy, as it was called, lasted only eleven years, but during that time it trained many of the subsequent leaders in the Baptist churches of New Jersey.* The Association also was responsible for adopting the Articles of Faith, popularly known as the Philadelphia Confession.** This strongly Calvinistic document was virtually the same as the Confession subscribed to by the English Baptists which in turn was dependent on the Westminster Confession. One of the most fruitful acts of the Association was the securing of support from its member churches for a missionary to travel among the settlements in the interior with an eye to the establishment of new Baptist churches. The wisdom of this action

* Nelson R. Burr, *Education in New Jersey 1630-1871* (Princeton, 1942), 150 ff.
** *Minutes of the Philadelphia Baptist Association* (Philadelphia, 1851), 46. See Henry C. Vedder, *A History of the Baptists in the Middle States* (Philadelphia, 1898), Chapter IV.

was attested by the rapid growth of frontier Baptist churches following the Revolution.

DIVERSITY AND TOLERANCE

As tension between the colonies and England gradually mounted, the religious life of New Jersey began to show some of the qualities which were to characterize it from then on. One of these was religious diversity. Even though the Anglicans tried hard to get a religious establishment such as they enjoyed in Virginia, and even though the Assembly had the power to create such an establishment, that power was never exercised. When Governor Cornbury proved to be unbelievably corrupt, the Anglican divines were forced to attack him, even though he was a strong supporter of religious uniformity. Thereafter, the other Royal governors, most of whom were also Anglican, seemed to favor religious diversity rather than uniformity so that eventually the concept of separation of church and state won out.* This does not mean that the various denominations were embued with a strong spirit of tolerance. They carried on verbal warfare and issued quantities of books and pamphlets against each other. But they seemed to recognize that seeking state aid in the fight would end in the loss of their own liberty. Thus they viewed the exclusion of government from church affairs in somewhat the same spirit as the Irish Republicans who watched the withdrawal of British troops from their shores with the comment, "Thank God they are gone; now we can fight in peace!"

While tolerance was not a notable virtue of the eighteenth-century Jerseyman, the very profusion of denominations in the Colony and the needs of the time forced many congregations into cooperative ventures which would have been impossible in New England or Virginia. Meetinghouses at Shrewsbury and Middletown, for in-

* Gordon Turner, "Church-State Relationships in Early New Jersey," *Proceedings of The New Jersey Historical Society*, LXIX, No. 3, 212-223.

stance, were used by both Congregationalists and Presbyterians, and the one in Middletown was also used by the Baptists. The Dutch Reformed and Scottish Presbyterians met for worship together in Freehold and Middletown.* This close association of different religious traditions led inevitably to a "live and let live" attitude on the part of the laity which the sectarianism of the clergy was never able to eradicate. For this reason they were not so inclined to acts of violence and cruelty against those with whom they disagreed as were the settlers in some of the other American colonies. As an example, while the people of New Jersey believed in witchcraft and witches fully as much as the New Englander and established the death penalty for them, so far as we know the penalty was never inflicted in New Jersey. Had they taken the matter seriously, one can imagine the horrifying results to come from an act such as the following from the General Assembly Minutes of East Jersey:

That all women of whatever age, rank, profession or degree, whether virgins, maids, or widows, who shall after this Act impose upon, seduce and betray into matrimony any of his Majesty's subjects by virtue of scents, cosmetics, washes, paints, artificial teeth, false hair, or high heeled shoes, shall incur the penalty of the law now in force against witchcraft and like misdemeanors.**

One further peculiarity of religion in New Jersey which began to appear about this time was what we have termed the New York–Philadelphia polarization. To a large extent, New Jersey was merely a thoroughfare between these two metropolitan centers. It is not strange, therefore, that power blocs arose in each area which aroused opposition elsewhere in the State. We can see this clearly in the case of the Presbyterians where the

* Nelson R. Burr, *The Anglican Church in New Jersey* (Philadelphia, 1954), 7.
* Quoted by C. S. Boyer, "Jersey Justice in Olden Days," *Proceedings of The New Jersey Historical Society*, XVI, No. 3, 265.

"Old Side" party became identified with Philadelphia and the "New Side" with New Brunswick. In the same way Frelinghuysen and Bertholf along the Raritan and Passaic rivers were opposed by the Collegiate churches of New York City. These were but portents of a condition that would eventually affect most of the New Jersey churches in the decades that lay ahead.

III

REVOLUTION AND RELIGION
1776-1835

W<small>HEN THE TENSION</small> between King and colonies which
had been building up for years finally broke into open
revolution, no colony was more deeply involved than
New Jersey, and no institution was more responsible for
this than the church. This is not to say that all churchmen favored revolt or supported the colonial government. On the contrary, there was a bitter division of
opinion cutting across communities and creating wounds
which took decades to heal. Generally speaking, those
who supported and those who opposed independence
were divided along denominational lines. The Presbyterians, Dutch Reformed, Baptists and Independent
groups for the most part were on the side of the Continental Congress, while the Anglicans, Methodists, and
Quakers supported the Crown, though for vastly differing
reasons. Even this, however, must be qualified, for there
were minorities within each church who disagreed with
the stand of their fellow members. Then, in addition,
there was a quite sizable portion of the American people
who favored whichever side was winning at the time.

Presbyterian Revolutionaries

Writing to Lord Dartmouth, Secretary of State in
charge of the American colonies, an English visitor in
New York gave his opinion of the colonial unrest: "Pres-

byterianism is really at the Bottom of this whole Conspiracy, has supplied it with Vigor, and will never rest, till something is decided upon it." * No doubt this was a vast exaggeration, but in New Jersey at least, there was much to substantiate the charge. More than half of the troops who followed Washington from New Jersey were Scotch-Irish Presbyterians, many of them recent immigrants to the Colony. Almost all the Presbyterian clergy supported the revolution after the die was cast, and the most influential speaker and writer in the State on behalf of independence was a Presbyterian teacher and clergyman: John Witherspoon. He occupied a crucial position as President of the College of New Jersey located at Princeton. After giving up a successful pastorate in Paisley, Scotland, he accepted the presidency of the young college, arriving there in 1768. The Presbyterian Church was not in a vigorous state at the time, because, despite the reunion of 1758, the differences between "Old Side" and "New Side" still remained. Princeton College, as the New Jersey College came to be called, was organized as a "New Side" institution, but the wealth and support which could make it effective was controlled by the "Old Side" churches of Philadelphia. One of the first accomplishments of Dr. Witherspoon was to commend himself to the Philadelphia clergy and thus bring the Presbyterian Church together in fact as well as in name. It was a fortunate development, not only for the future of the college, but especially for the church. With the longstanding tensions between the north Jersey and south Jersey sections of the church now largely overcome, the Presbyterians could turn their undivided attention to the crisis in colonial affairs posed by George III and his government.

It was not until 1774 that Witherspoon took any active role in political affairs, though he already had shown his colonial sympathies by permitting his students to demon-

* Ambrose Serle to William, Lord Dartmouth, Nov. 8, 1776, as quoted by Leonard Lundin, *Cockpit of the Revolution* (Princeton, 1940), 100.

strate against the hated tax on tea and in support of the Boston insurgents. During the summer, when plans were underway for a meeting of the Continental Congress, Witherspoon wrote an essay entitled, "Thoughts on American Liberty," which gave his views on the purpose of holding the Congress and suggested some courses of action. It was an important document and helped to mold the temper of the Congress when it met in Philadelphia. Beginning with a profession of loyalty to the King and of reluctance to break the ties with Britain, Witherspoon urged the Congress to make very clear that the colonies would not tolerate the tyrannical acts of the Crown, that they would prefer war and extermination to slavery. In addition, he urged that steps be taken to unite the colonies so that whatever action they took would be united action. While he professed a repugnance to revolution, he urged Congress to prepare for the worst by organizing the colonial militia, encouraging domestic manufacture, and boycotting British imports.

The following summer at the meeting of the Synod of New York and Philadelphia a pastoral letter was sent from the Synod to all the Presbyterian churches in the Middle Colonies. News of the bloodshed at Lexington and Concord had already enflamed the passions of the colonists to a serious pitch, so it is surprising to find the pastoral letter urging continued loyalty to the King and avoidance of insulting language when speaking of him. At the same time the Synod asked for full support of the Continental Congress as representing the best expression of colonial sentiments. Further, the letter advised "that a spirit of candour, charity, and mutual esteem, be preserved and promoted towards those of different religious denominations." * Witherspoon served as chairman of the committee which drew up the letter, and considering that he was already one of the members elected to represent New Jersey in the Continental Congress, the re-

* *Records of the Presbyterian Church in the U.S.A.*, 467, 468. Quoted by Charles A. Briggs, *American Presbyterianism* (New York, 1885), 350.

straint and dignity of the epistle attests to the maturity and responsibility both of the good doctor and his Presbyterian colleagues. While there were some Presbyterians, especially in Pennsylvania, who opposed the radical steps taken by the Congress, once the Declaration of Independence was signed the Presbyterians swung their support to the Revolutionary cause almost to a man.* Witherspoon was the only clergyman to sign the Declaration, and thereafter he served as a member of the Congress until the war was over. Further, there were more graduates of Princeton who signed the Declaration than of Harvard and Yale combined, even though Princeton was the youngest of the three schools.

The reward for this bold stand was not long in coming. British troops on Long Island burned Witherspoon in effigy, and as they marched through New Jersey they marked Presbyterian churches for desecration and destruction. A number of churches, such as the ones at Mount Holly and Elizabethtown, were burned to the ground. The church at Newtown was turned into a prison and guardhouse. At Princeton the Hessians tore up the church furniture for firewood and used the building as a troop garrison. Nor did the Princeton College buildings escape the general devastation. As a sign of contempt, the British employed the basement of Nassau Hall as a stable, burnt the wooden furnishings, and destroyed or carried away most of the library.** Other churches in New Jersey were used as stables also, the accumulated filth from the horses being left on the floor when the British moved out. Many of the Presbyterian clergy became chaplains in the Continental Army, and not a few, like the Reverend James Caldwell of Elizabethtown, paid with their lives for their service. Caldwell is renowned for supplying Watts' Psalm Books from a nearby Presbyterian church to the troops when their supply of wadding

* Cf. Leonard J. Trinterud, *The Forming of an American Tradition* (Philadelphia, 1949), 246-250.
** Varnum L. Collins, *President Witherspoon* (Princeton, 1925), II, 93-97.

ran low. Coming out with a handful of books he passed them out with the cry, "Now boys, give them Watts!" Caldwell's wife had been murdered by a British soldier and he himself was shot by a drunken sentinel.

DUTCH REFORMED PATRIOTS

Though not as numerous as the Presbyterians, the Dutch Reformed contributed more than their fair share to the Revolutionary cause. Both because of their national bias and their concern for liberty, most of them were as strongly anti-British as were the Scots. On the banks of the Raritan, in the church made famous by Dominie Frelinghuysen, the pastor during the war years was the Reverend Doctor Jacob R. Hardenburgh, a strong patriot who preached such vigorous sermons against the British that they offered a reward of one hundred pounds for his arrest. The good dominie protested perfect confidence in the providence of God, but he also never went to sleep without a loaded musket at his side. During the winter of 1778-1779, General Washington and his troops encamped near the Reformed Church and struck up a friendship with the Dutch which led the consistory of the congregation to send a letter to the General pledging their complete support for his cause, to which Washington gave a courteous reply.* Later on the British burned the church out of reprisal for the Dutch support of the Revolution. Farther to the south the pastor of the Reformed Church of Millstone had his church burned and narrowly escaped with his life as the British went through his house with swords and bayonets, piercing every place where he might be hiding. Dr. Dirck Romeyn, after preaching most of the men of his congregation into the army, was forced to flee when the British came and destroyed his house. And the Reverend Benjamin Du Bois of Monmouth County actually shouldered knapsack and gun and went out on

* Abraham Messler, *First Things in Old Somerset* (Somerville, 1899), 52-53.

patrol with the Continental troops. Needless to say, the Dutch churches received no better treatment from their British captors than the Scottish churches did.*

BAPTIST INVOLVEMENT

Because the Baptist churches were for the most part small, struggling congregations scattered along the Delaware River as far south as Cape May and up around Piscataway, there is little record of their involvement in the Revolution. While the memory of Anglican persecution made many Baptists anti-British, there were others who favored the Tory cause. Deep differences of opinion cut across the Baptist congregations of Middletown and Upper Freehold as to which side should be supported. Abel Morgan tried to take a mediating position at first, and he remained in the Middletown Church throughout the war. Baptist pastors such as David Jones, however, spoke out warmly from the pulpit on behalf of the Revolution. Three Baptist ministers from New Jersey served as chaplains in the Continental Army, and many Baptist laymen distinguished themselves as fighters for the Colonial cause. One of them, John Hart of Hopewell, was a signer of the Declaration of Independence.**

The minutes of the Baptist Association, on the other hand, scarcely paid any note to the war except to urge upon its members fasting and prayer, for

our continent is filled with tears and blood, ravages and desolation abound, perpetrated by English troops, and, if possible, by more wicked combinations of base traitors among ourselves, as now it is, when religion declines, and iniquity triumphs.†

* John A. Todd, *Reformed (Dutch) Church in America: the Posture of its Ministers and People During the Revolution* (New York, 1877), 26-29.

** Norman Maring, *A History of New Jersey Baptists* (Unpublished MS held by New Jersey Baptist Convention, East Orange), Chapter II, 36-39. Cf. Louis H. Patterson, "John Hart, the New Jersey Signer," *Proceedings of The New Jersey Historical Society*, X, No. 4, 375-382.

† *Minutes of the Philadelphia Baptist Association, 1707-1807* (Philadelphia, 1881), 168.

While the annual Circular Letter which went out from the Association to all the member congregations dealt almost exclusively with personal piety and theological matters, the fact that the place of meeting of the Association twice had to be changed and that, in 1777, the meeting was abandoned altogether shows that the war hampered the religious life of the Baptists, as indeed it did that of all the churches.

ANGLICANS: A HOUSE DIVIDED

Contrasting sharply with the Presbyterians, Dutch Reformed, and Baptists were the Anglicans, Methodists, and Quakers. The Anglicans, of course, were sturdy supporters of the Crown throughout the war. With but few exceptions, their clergy actively opposed the Continental Congress and the Revolution. For them the struggle was much more than political; it was ecclesiastical, doctrinal, and liturgical as well. The Anglican priests were nearly all Englishmen, born and bred, who still regarded America as missionary soil. Not only were they drawn to England by family ties, but their financial support was largely English as well, through the Society for the Propagation of the Gospel in Foreign Parts. They were convinced that the Anglican Church was the only true church in the colonies, and that the goal of their ministry should be the creation of a religious establishment in America similar to the church-state union in England. It was this which gave added impetus to their demand for an Anglican bishop in the colonies. In 1760 the Anglican clergy petitioned Governor Thomas Boone to forbid justices of the peace to perform marriages, and when the Governor replied that he did not have the power to make such a change, the angry priests appealed to the Bishop of London. The Anglicans claimed that their concern was to add dignity and reverence to the marriage rite, but their opponents interpreted it as an additional sign that the Church of England was grasping for more power and financial reward.* The very fact that

* Cf. *New Jersey Archives*, IX, 504 and Nelson R. Burr, *The Anglican Church in New Jersey* (Philadelphia, 1954), 178-180.

each week the Book of Common Prayer prescribed prayers for the King, the Royal Family, and Parliament gave convincing testimony to where Anglican loyalties lay. This was also attested by the fact that when hostilities erupted most of the Anglican clergy returned to England or took refuge behind the British lines rather than alter their liturgy or their allegiance.

The unanimity of the clergy, on the other hand, was not necessarily reflected among the laity. Professor W. W. Sweet has pointed out the interesting fact that the loyalty of the Anglican laity to the King was in inverse ratio to their strength in the colonies. In Virginia and Maryland where the Anglicans were strongest, the smallest proportion of Tories was found. But in New England where the Anglicans were a very small part of the population they were Tory almost to a man. New Jersey, which had a fair-sized Anglican population, witnessed a division of the laity about evenly between Whigs and Tories.* This was a source of embarrassment and regret to their priests who worked mightily to forward the British cause. None was more outstanding in this than the Reverend Jonathan Odell, rector of St. Mary's in Burlington. Odell was one of the few native Jerseymen among the Episcopal clergy. His mother was the daughter of Jonathan Dickinson, the first president of the College of New Jersey. Odell graduated from the college (now moved to Princeton) and became a surgeon. Later he sailed to England to train for holy orders and finally returned to New Jersey as a priest. During the war he wrote satiric verse against the Revolutionary leaders which was used by the British for propaganda purposes. Washington and Witherspoon were two who received special attention:

Hear thy indictment, Washington, at large;
Attend and listen to the solemn charge;
Thou has supported an atrocious cause
Against the King, thy country, and the laws;

* William W. Sweet, *Religion in the Development of American Culture* (New York, 1952), 14.

Myriads of wives and fathers at thy hand
Their slaughtered husbands, slaughtered sons demand

Meanwhile unhappy Jersey mourns her thrall;
Ordained by the vilest of the vile to fall;
To fall by Witherspoon!—O name the curse
Of sound religion, and disgrace of verse.

I've known him seek the dungeon, dark as night,
Imprison'd Tories to convert or fright;
While to myself I've hummed in dismal tune,
I'd rather be a dog than Witherspoon.*

He also became involved in espionage work, serving as a link between Benedict Arnold and the British authorities when Arnold offered to surrender West Point.

By 1781, however, most of the Anglican clergy had been forced to flee their parishes. Some of them became chaplains in the British service, and the rest returned to England. Of the eleven priests in New Jersey in 1774 only four remained. One was intermittently insane, another was a drunkard, and a third gave up the use of the Book of Common Prayer in public worship. Only one, Abraham Beach of New Brunswick, retained his Anglican ties yet continued to remain near his parish church. Since he refused to omit the offending prayers from the liturgy, he had to keep the church closed during most of the war.** Eventually, he bowed to the inevitable and began worship services again, but without the objectionable prayers. Mention should be made of one priest, Robert Blackwell of Gloucester County, who threw in his lot with the Revolutionaries. He became chaplain and surgeon to the First Pennsylvania Brigade during the time the Continental Army was wintering at Valley Forge.

* Winthrop Sargent, *Loyalist Poetry of the Revolution,* I, 9, quoted in Sweet, *Religion in the Development of American Culture* (New York, 1952), 20.
** Nelson R. Burr, *The Anglican Church in New Jersey* (Philadelphia, 1954), 416.

Even though the Methodists had already gone far in breaking away from the Anglican Church by the time war began, the Methodist leaders were predominantly Tory. John Wesley, who was not uncritical of British treatment of the colonies at first, had his mind changed by a pamphlet written by Samuel Johnson, "Taxation no Tyranny." From then on Wesley opposed the Revolution and strongly urged his followers in America to remain neutral and not oppose the King. Neutrality, of course, was an impossibility as soon as fighting broke out, so all the English preachers whom Wesley had sent over went back to England, with the exception of Francis Asbury. The attitude of the Methodist leaders naturally made the whole Methodist movement suspect as far as the Americans were concerned, and if Asbury had left, there is a good chance that Methodism in America might have disappeared altogether. Asbury, whose extensive travels through the colonies had given him a keen insight into the colonial mind, wrote in his Journal on March 19, 1776:

I also received an affectionate letter from Mr. Wesley, and am truly sorry that the venerable man ever dipped into the politics of America. My desire is to live in love and peace with all men; to do them no harm, but all the good I can. However, it discovers Mr. Wesley's conscientious attachment to the government under which he lived. Had he been a subject of America, no doubt but he would have been as zealous an advocate of the American cause. But some inconsiderate persons have taken occasion to censure the Methodists in America, on account of Mr. Wesley's political sentiments.*

As it turned out, the stand of John Wesley eventually proved to be a boon. By calling them, "poor deluded rebels in America," ** he cut the tie which bound them

* Francis Asbury, *Journal and Letters of Francis Asbury* (London, 1958), I, 181.
** John Wesley, *Journal*, Aug. 1, 1777 (London, 1916), VI, 167.

to the English branch of the Church, so that when the War ended American Methodism was free to develop its own forms and institutions without interference from abroad. The immediate effect, however, was almost disastrous. During the first year of the war Methodist membership in New Jersey was cut in half and by 1779 numbered only 140. For a time Trenton was the only circuit and Daniel Ruff the only appointed preacher.* The flight of all Wesley's preachers, except Asbury, the label "Tory" which the Methodists now had to bear, and the havoc in New Jersey wreaked by the war itself, undid the work of decades. Even Francis Asbury found he could not ride freely anymore, because he refused to take an oath of allegiance to the new regime, and most of the states required such an oath. Fortunately, Delaware did not, so Asbury found refuge there where he impatiently waited out the end of the war. Gradually, things began to improve. Daniel Ruff was joined by Benjamin Abbott, who traveled widely through West Jersey preaching wherever he could and reviving some of the defunct classes there. George Mair was preaching in East Jersey by 1780 and the following year the annual Conference reported over five hundred members, almost doubling the number of the previous year.

QUAKER NON-RESISTANCE

In New Jersey the largest religious body to oppose the Revolution was the Society of Friends, though the reasons for their opposition differed sharply from those of the Anglicans. At first glance this appears strange in light of the fact that the Quakers had suffered cruelly at the hands of the British Establishment and would therefore be naturally disposed to favor freedom. That the Friends appreciated the freedom to worship as they pleased was, of course, obvious. Ever since the time of George Fox they had supported religious toleration and separation of

* Nelson R. Burr, *The Anglican Church in New Jersey* (Philadelphia, 1954), 322.

church and state. At the same time, they were pacifists. As long as the Colonies continued to appeal for redress from their wrongs, the Quakers made their voice heard also. But when recourse to arms became the policy, then they had to abstain for conscience' sake. It was not an easy thing to do because by this time Quakers had built up sizable fortunes in the mercantile business. They had a considerable interest in the question over taxation and representation. Yet when the non-importation agreements were made among the colonies, most of the Quaker merchants cooperated. Unfortunately, however, the Quakers not only had scruples against war but against revolution as well. When England had been subjected to plots and counterplots during the seventeenth century, the Friends had resolutely stayed out of them, for as an old Quaker document of 1696 put it, "The setting up and putting down Kings and governments is God's peculiar prerogative, for causes best known to himself." * So the Friends felt it necessary to dissociate themselves from anything resembling revolution.

There was a difference of opinion among the Friends about how far these regulations need go. All of them were agreed that offensive war was unchristian and therefore out of the question for a good Quaker. But defensive war was, to some of them, justifiable. The man who expounded this theory most forcefully was James Logan. He was not able to win support for his views in the Yearly Meeting, but he did gain a following among some of the younger Quakers of Philadelphia. Most of the Quakers, however, kept to the stricter ruling. Not only did they refuse to take part in the fighting or support it by their taxes or gifts, but they were forbidden to take part in the Revolutionary government in any way. They allowed their homes and goods to be pillaged by the foraging armies, they gave up their houses to quarter soldiers, at the same time being accused of treason by both sides for refusal to cooperate. By bitter experience many of them

* Quoted by Rufus Jones, *The Quakers in the American Colonies* (London, 1911), 563.

discovered that neutrality in wartime is simply impossible. As the city of Philadelphia and the surrounding areas on the Jersey side changed hands with the shifting fortunes of war, the Quaker inhabitants were subjected to all kinds of harrassment. Several were hanged on the charge of treason. Others were imprisoned. Still others were impoverished by costly fines or expropriations. Yet through it all, most of the Quakers remained true to their convictions. A few who were disowned by the various monthly meetings for support of the Revolution formed themselves into the Society of Free Quakers, but it was always a small group and died out after the war. Not until peace was finally declared and the British had gone, did the Quakers as a whole accept the new government as the lawfully constituted one over them.

By the time the war came to an end there was scarcely a hamlet or town in New Jersey which had escaped some form of military intrusion. The State was a natural passage between New York City and Philadelphia, so that it was always in a condition of siege. The vast majority of its people actively supported the Revolution as seen by the fact that the State contributed no less than nine thousand men to the Revolutionary Army out of a total of seventy-three thousand from all the colonies. This was one-eighth of the total even though New Jersey's population was less than one-twentieth that of all the rest. When you exclude the Quakers and other conscientious objectors, 46 per cent of the remaining male population bore arms in the State.* At the same time there were many who were Tory in sympathy and they were fairly well distributed across the State. This led to fratricidal strife in many a hamlet and town as Tories and Whigs exchanged verbal tirades which often led to open violence. Near Pompton a group of patriots erected a "liberty pole" which was shortly cut down by Tories. Several times the pole was replaced only to be cut down again

* Cornelius C. Vermeule, "Number of Soldiers in the Revolution," *Proceedings of The New Jersey Historical Society*, VII, No. 3, 223-227.

until finally the patriots put up a pole defended with "bars of iron" and on the pole wrote "Liberty, Prosperity and no Popery." * Such symbols appeared in many localities and often gave rise to open clashes between those who supported the American cause and those who supported the King.

Post-War Reorganization

War is always costly. The Revolution left not only death and material destruction in its wake, but it left the survivors spent both mentally and emotionally. Just at the time that new energy and creative effort were most needed to rebuild the ruins left by the fighting, everyone discovered how exhausted he was. Consequently the prevailing temper, as in every postwar period, was a compound of cynicism, moral lethargy, and despair. It is scarcely necessary to point out what effect this had on the religious concerns of the time. Those who called most fervently on the God of battles suddenly ceased calling on any god at all. The decline in religious interest immediately affected the life of the organized churches. Most of the citizens of the State appear to have been outside the membership of any church, and among the educated leaders many had adopted the spirit of the English deists and French *philosophes* which regarded the institution of the church as a social irrelevancy at best. When peace finally came to America, each church group faced the problem of repairing the damage done by the war. In addition each church had special problems of its own which demanded solution, not least of which was adjusting its life to conditions in the newly created independent union, the United States of America. How the various denominations met this challenge determined to a large degree their growth in the nineteenth century.

No group faced a more difficult prospect in this connection than did the Anglicans. Largely bereft of clergy,

* G. C. Schenck, "Early Settlements and Settlers of Pompton, Pequannoc and Pompton Plains," *Proceedings of The New Jersey Historical Society*, New Series, IV, Nos. 1-4, 85.

called "traitors" for their support of the King during the Revolution, cut off from financial support, and without any ready means for securing either clergy or money, the wonder is that they survived as a church at all. Many of the parishes had disbanded, and those that remained were almost demoralized by the outcome of the War. Fortunately, there was one man who was willing to assume a leading role in rebuilding the church. Abraham Beach, Rector of Christ Church in New Brunswick, had been forced into relative inactivity during the war years, but with the coming of peace he set about the task of revitalizing the denomination. Two problems of crucial importance had to be faced at the onset. First, the Episcopal leaders in all the states had to be gathered together to consider the formation of a national church, and second, they had to face the question of securing a bishop. Beach began corresponding at once with Episcopal clergy in New England and in the southern states as well as those closer to home. In March, 1783, he met with 17 other priests in New York City to frame an appeal to the Anglican hierarchy in England for a bishop. The discussions there brought out a sharp difference of opinion between the northern and southern clergy. The New England clergy were quite conservative in their outlook and tended to be "High Church." To them the most pressing responsibility was the securing of a bishop. As far as they were concerned, nothing else could be done until the episcopal question was settled.

The southern part of the church, on the other hand, was more liberal in outlook and tended to be "Low Church." Representative of this viewpoint was Dr. William White, Rector of Christ Church in Philadelphia. In 1782 he wrote a pamphlet, "The Case of the Episcopal Church Considered," in which he suggested that priests be non-episcopally ordained if a bishop could not be secured soon. With this view, which would involve a radical reorganization of church polity, the southern clergy were largely in sympathy. Furthermore, the clergy in the various states were making plans to organize along state lines regardless of what the other states were doing.

Alarmed by this development, Beach wrote to White suggesting a meeting in New Brunswick to see whether a union of all Episcopal churches in the United States of America could be established and to air some of the differences that were dividing the Church. Once again New Jersey became both a rallying point and a battleground for church opinion. The meeting which convened at Beach's own church during May, 1784, was important in several respects. It proved impossible to agree on any principles of union, because of the sharp differences on the episcopacy expressed by the northern and southern branches of the church. It was evident further, that with the separation from England, the church had become virtually congregational in polity. Two decisions were ultimately made: to call another interstate meeting in October of that year and, more important, to associate the laity along with the clergy in the decision-making assemblies of the church.*

Meanwhile, the question of a bishop was being handled separately by the Episcopal clergy of Connecticut. They selected Samuel Seabury, who had served some years before as a missionary priest in New Brunswick, to be consecrated as their first bishop. Seabury took ship for England to secure Episcopal orders and thus raised afresh a controversy that had been going on for nearly half a century. Long before the Revolutionary War broke out, the Anglican priests had agitated for a bishop of their own. At the same time the Independents and Presbyterians had bitterly opposed the idea, because of the political implications involved. A notable battle of the press had ensued between Thomas Chandler, rector in Elizabethtown, and Charles Chauncey, the testy Boston Congregationalist.** If anything, this only strengthened opposition to an American bishop. Oddly enough, the

* Nelson R. Burr, *The Anglican Church in New Jersey* (Philadelphia, 1954), 417-420.
** Cf. Arthur L. Cross, *The Anglican Episcopate and the American Colonies* (New York, 1902), Chapter 7; Carl Bridenbaugh, *Mitre and Scepter* (New York, 1962), *passim*.

English hierarchy was almost as opposed to the idea as were the American dissenters. The English bishops regarded themselves as lords and lived as such with palaces, coaches, and servants. The idea of missionary bishops in the wilds of America was to most English churchmen as fantastic as, in the words of a recent historian, "a plan to ask our government to send a symphony orchestra to the natives of Guam." * Also at issue was the fact that Seabury could not take an oath of allegiance to the Crown even though it was considered a necessary part of the consecration ceremony, since he would be serving in a country which had just won its freedom from that allegiance by force of arms. It is not surprising, then, that when Seabury arrived in London for consecration, he was politely but definitely refused. At last, after a year of waiting, he traveled to Scotland where he was given a sympathetic hearing by the non-juring bishops of the Scottish Episcopal Church. These bishops were successors to the men who had refused to take the oath of allegiance to William and Mary following the Glorious Revolution of 1688, and therefore they could sympathize with Seabury's refusal to take a similar oath to George III. In November, 1784, Seabury was consecrated by three Scottish bishops and shortly afterward returned to America.

Before Seabury returned, plans were well underway for a General Convention representing the Episcopal churches in all the American states, which finally met in Philadelphia during the early fall of 1785. The middle and southern states were well represented, but the New England clergy and Bishop Seabury refused to attend. The division between the conservative north and the liberal south was still very much of a reality. It was not until 1789 that the two sections finally came together to create the Protestant Episcopal Church in the United States, and much of the credit for the union must go to the clergy of New Jersey. They shared many of the conservative views of the Connecticut clergy. When the

* J. T. Addison, *The Episcopal Church in the United States, 1789-1931* (New York, 1951), 55.

proposal for a radical revision of the Book of Common Prayer was made, the Jersey delegates opposed it, and the revision was ultimately abandoned. Finally, the only changes retained were the prayers for the new government to replace prayers for the King. In 1815 New Jersey received its own bishop in the person of the Reverend John Croes, Rector of Christ Church in New Brunswick. It was not an easy burden that he assumed. The Episcopal Church was still very small and its Tory past was still held against it. As late as 1830 there were only 33 congregations and 900 communicant members in the State, and these were chiefly clustered around Newark, Perth Amboy, Trenton, and Burlington. Even after his consecration, Bishop Croes continued on as rector in New Brunswick, because the diocese had no salary for its bishop.*

METHODISTS CREATE A NATIONAL CHURCH

Up to the end of the Revolutionary War the Methodists were considered to be a part of the Church of England, and so they shared some of the odium heaped on the Anglicans. But the Methodists were able to regain public confidence more quickly than their Episcopal brethren, and they were the first denomination to establish a national church in this country. This was made possible by a number of events both prior and subsequent to the war. The flight of all John Wesley's preachers, except Asbury, meant that during the War the leadership of the church was almost entirely indigenous and thus free of the accusation that they were under British control. During this period Asbury quietly took over the reins of command so that when peace came nearly all the Methodist preachers in the colonies looked to him for leadership. Fearful that Wesley might wish to send over someone else to superintend the work, one of the preachers wrote him in 1783:

* Nelson R. Burr, *The Anglican Church in N. J.* (Philadelphia, 1954), 460.

The preachers are united to Mr. Asbury, and esteem him highly in love for his work's sake; and earnestly desire his continuance on the continent . . . to act as he does at present, (to wit) to superintend the whole work, and go through all the circuits once a year.*

Wesley wisely grasped the situation and set about devising some sort of organization for the American Methodists which would allow them to develop along lines best suited to their national independence. It was fortunate he did, because trouble on this score had already risen. A group of preachers in Virginia had gathered during the war to organize an independent Methodist church in which they would celebrate the sacraments even though they were not ordained. Asbury was able to prevent a schism and prevail upon the impatient Virginians to wait for word from Wesley before taking action, but they were not willing to wait much longer after the war. Wesley had already given some thought to the problem, especially since the Anglican priests had refused to care for his followers. Finally, to the great disgust of his brother Charles, John became convinced that as a presbyter he had the right to ordain. When he discovered that Alexandrian bishops had been consecrated by presbyters in the early Church, that was enough to determine his next course of action. Calling in Dr. Thomas Coke, another Anglican priest turned Methodist, Wesley ordained him Superintendent of the Methodist societies in America. Though the title was "Superintendent" it carried with it episcopal powers and was so understod by Coke. In addition Wesley prepared a "Sunday Service," a hymnbook, and a revision of the Thirty-nine Articles for use in the American Church.

Coke and two companions landed in New York late in 1784 and at once made contact with Asbury. Together they planned the famous "Christmas Conference" in Baltimore which created the Methodist Episcopal Church.

* William W. Sweet, *Religion on the American Frontier:* Volume IV, *The Methodists* (Chicago, 1946), 13.

At this conference Asbury was ordained Superintendent to serve with Coke, though it was clear to everyone from the start that Asbury would be the dominant figure. The two superintendents ordained the more capable preachers as deacons and elders and established the criteria by which the two orders might be conferred in the future. Despite an abortive effort on the part of Coke a few years later to effect a reunion between the Methodist and Episcopal churches, the two were now completely separate. The Methodists began to spread with amazing rapidity, once their independence was assured. In 1789, at the shrewd suggestion of Asbury, a letter was written to President Washington shortly after his inauguration, expressing "the warm feelings of our hearts, and our sincere congratulations, on your appointment to the presidentship of these states." The letter was signed by Coke and Asbury as bishops of the Methodist Episcopal Church and presented to Washington in person by Asbury. Washington replied with a letter of thanks in which he promised to "implore the Divine benediction on yourselves and your religious community." * Such a testimonial did much to dispel the charge that the Methodists were not patriotic, a fact which was given wide publicity by their itinerant preachers.

It was in south Jersey that Methodism made its greatest advance. The mobility of the circuit system, the informality of its worship, the joyous quality of its hymnody appealed to rural inhabitants and made possible the establishment of chapels where other denominations hesitated to penetrate. Even more important, the practice of training preachers during the course of their ministerial service meant that the Methodists could expand the number of their ministers much more rapidly than either the Presbyterians or the Episcopalians. When Benjamin Abbott began itinerating near Trenton in 1778 there were scarcely one hundred and fifty Methodists in the

* *Journal and Letters of Francis Asbury* (London: 1958), III, 70-72.

State. Seven years later there were 1028 members organized into three circuits, and by 1830 they had overtaken the Presbyterians with over fifteen thousand five hundred members.* Such rapid growth was not without its problems. Bishop Asbury, not only supervised the church; he ran it. Among his most important powers was the location of the various preachers in each conference to their stations or circuits. No appeal was permitted from his decision in this matter. It was almost inevitable that grumbling and charges of autocracy were heard, and finally a motion was made at the Baltimore Conference in 1792 that if any preacher felt himself aggrieved in his location he could appeal to the conference, and if the conference upheld him the bishop would be obliged to appoint him to another circuit. The motion was defeated after long debate only to be succeeded by an appeal for lay representation in the councils of the church.

Each year the question of autocratic government was raised in one form or another, and in 1821 William S. Stockton, a prominent Methodist layman began publishing a journal in Trenton, *The Wesleyan Repository*. It soon became a sounding board for the various groups who sought more democracy in the Church. The bishops were adamant, however, and the problem was not solved until 1828, when a group of dissidents broke away and later formed the Methodist Protestant Church. Three of the leaders in this division, Asa Shinn, Samuel Jennings, and Thomas Stockton, son of the publisher, came originally from New Jersey. The Methodist Protestant Church never became very strong in the State, but by the middle of the century it had a New Jersey Conference.** The Methodist Protestant split was but one of many divisions within Methodism to come later.

* Nelson R. Burr, *The Anglican Church in New Jersey* (Philadelphia, 1954), 328-329. See William T. Hanzsche, "History of the Churches in New Jersey," *The Story of New Jersey* (New York, 1945), II, 311.
** Cf. Ancel H. Bassett, *A Concise History of the Methodist Protestant Church from its Origin* (Pittsburgh, 1882).

SAGE LIBRARY HALL.   HERTZOG HALL.   SUYDAM HALL.

THEOLOGICAL SEMINARY OF THE REFORMED CHURCH IN AMERICA, AT NEW BRUNSWICK, N. J.

Wood cut of New Brunswick Theological Seminary, c. 1875
*From Centennial of The Theological Seminary of The
Reformed Church in America, New York, 1885*

Among the smaller church bodies in New Jersey, the Dutch Reformed Church was so preoccupied with internal problems that there was neither energy nor desire to expand. Just before war broke out, the Church had solved the Coetus-Conferentie dispute which had divided the denomination for sixteen years.

The Coetus party had sought for a certain degree of freedom from the strict control of the Dutch judicatory in Amsterdam, while the ultra-conservative Conferentie party insisted on leaving absolute control overseas. The plan of union enabled the Church to set up its own judicatories independent of the Netherlands. Further advance, however, was prevented by the onset of hostilities during which the Dutch churches suffered repeated attacks, and many of them were destroyed during the course of the war. The most pressing problem facing the Church when peace came was the training of a qualified ministry. Accordingly the General Synod of 1784 elected John Henry Livingston as professor of theology to instruct suitable candidates. At first Dr. Livingston, who was the pastor of the Collegiate Reformed Church in New York City, conducted classes in his own home, later moving to a house in Brooklyn. Finally, he went to New Brunswick in 1810 where the New Brunswick Seminary, the oldest theological seminary in America, has remained ever since. Also located at New Brunswick was Queen's College, organized in 1766 by ministers and laymen of the Dutch Reformed Church, though not very active until after the Revolution.

As Queen's College was hardly an appropriate name for an American institution after independence was secured, Rutgers College was later substituted, in honor of Colonel Henry Rutgers, whose benefactions had enriched the school. Despite these advances, the Dutch Church failed to grow very rapidly. It was still too closely associated with one national group to be easily Americanized. Even a modest attempt to bring the worship of the church more in line with the needs of the New World resulted in a schism in 1822 when a splinter group called the True Dutch Reformed Church * came into being.

Lutheran Beginnings

Since the Swedes had colonized in southern New Jersey, there had not been many other Lutheran congregations established. Some Dutch Lutherans had settled in Hackensack and along the Raritan toward the end of the seventeenth century. Later they were joined by German Lutherans who helped support the few Lutheran churches in the area. Unhappily, it was very difficult to secure pastors, and those sent out by the German ministerium left much to be desired. Not until the great missionary pastor, Henry Melchior Muhlenberg, began visitation among the Germans in New Jersey did the Lutheran cause brighten in that State. He was able to settle a violent dispute among the four German congregations along the Raritan River and later procured a pastor for them. He also organized schools in each locality where churches were found and placed schoolmasters there. The education was admittedly rather meager, being chiefly catechetical instruction, but at least the children learned to read and write, which was a distinct advantage.** Muhlenberg also served the German congregations in Hackensack and in Cohansey to the south. Until his death in 1787 he continued to travel through eastern Pennsylvania and New Jersey teaching, preaching, administering the sacraments, and keeping peace in the churches. Thanks to his patient shepherding, the Lutheran churches were well established and survived the war intact, even though they did not grow in numbers until somewhat later.†

* Cf. William C. Kiessel, Jr., "Dr. Solomon Froeligh" *Proceedings of The New Jersey Historical Society*, LXXIII, No. 1, 28-40 and Jacob Brinkerhoff, *The History of the True Reformed Dutch Church in the U.S.A.* (New York, 1873).

** Henry M. Muhlenberg, *Journals* (Philadelphia, 1942), I.

† Cf. John C. Honeyman, "Zion, St. Paul and Other Early Lutheran Churches in Central N. J.," *Proceedings of The New Jersey Historical Society*, New Series, IX-XVI, *passim*.

There were few Roman Catholics in New Jersey until after the Revolution. Despite the guarantee of religious freedom in East and West Jersey, this freedom was specifically denied Catholics as soon as the State became a Royal Colony. Even though official toleration had been continued, the violent antipathy of most of the colonial settlers to Romanism in any form would have made widespread Catholic penetration difficult. Of the few Catholics who did settle in the Jerseys, most kept their religion to themselves and eventually joined another church or made no profession at all. During the middle of the eighteenth century, Father Theodore Schneider, a Jesuit who lived in Philadelphia, made brief forays into New Jersey visiting German Catholics in Salem County. Later Ferdinand Steinmeyer, better known as Father Farmer, made regular visits to scattered Catholic families along the Delaware and over to the Raritan.* Mass was celebrated in private homes with as little publicity as possible.

During the Revolution a number of Catholics distinguished themselves in the colonial cause such as Charles Carroll, delegate from Maryland to the Continental Congress, John Barry, outstanding naval officer, and Stephen Moylan, muster master-general on Washington's staff.** As a result of this support some of the animosity toward the Catholics began to disappear, but this only accentuated another awkward fact: the American Catholics were technically under the supervision of the Vicar Apostolic of London, an ardent Englishman.

Obviously such a condition could not continue. The Vatican considered for a time placing the American Church under a French bishop, but the priests in this country strongly objected. The man chiefly responsible for bringing some order to the scattered Catholic missions

* John G. Shea. *The Catholic Church in Colonial Days* (New York, 1886), 389 f. and 448 f.
** John T. Ellis, *American Catholicism* (Chicago, 1956), 37.

was John Carroll, a priest from a socially prominent family in Maryland. He had already shown administrative ability and great tact in handling people, so he was chosen by his fellow priests as their choice to head the Catholics in the United States. None other than Benjamin Franklin, then representing his country in Paris, supported Carroll's promotion, with the result that the priest was made Prefect Apostolic for the American Church and in 1790 was consecrated as its first bishop. It was not until 1814 that New Jersey got its first Catholic Church, a simple frame-building in Trenton dedicated as the Church of St. John. Within the next seventeen years four more churches were built, and Bishop Carroll traveled faithfully among them until a diocesan reorganization divided New Jersey between the dioceses of New York and Philadelphia. Growth was still very slow until the great waves of immigration brought workers from Catholic countries to the State several decades later.

PRESBYTERIANISM VERSUS RATIONALISM

The denomination which emerged from the Revolution in the most advantageous condition was undoubtedly the Presbyterian. The Presbyterians had been self-governing for almost a century so the war did not involve broken ties with a mother church as it did for most of the other church bodies. Because of their united stand on behalf of the colonies, they had gained considerable prestige throughout the State. In addition they were fortunate in possessing many able leaders who served the State as well as the church with distinction. The chief task confronting the Presbyterians upon the cessation of hostilities was to create a national organization suitable to the needs of an expanding church. The Synod of New York and Philadelphia had from its origin, included all the ministers and an equal number of elders from the constituent presbyteries. With churches now scattered over a wide area, this was too cumbersome an organization to handle the work of the church effectively. Accordingly, a new constitution was drawn up dividing the sixteen presbyteries among four synods and creating a general assembly with proportional representation from the presbyteries. In addition the Westminster Confession was altered to remove the references to an established church and to endorse the idea of freedom of worship for all Christian bodies. In 1789 the General Assembly was constituted and the Church was ready to face other serious problems.

The times were not propitious for religion. The devastation caused by the War and the inflation afterward brought serious economic hardship throughout New Jersey. As the largest church body in the State, the Presbyterians were especially hard hit. Many congregations, unable to pay their ministers, melted away as countless Jerseymen moved west in search of a better livelihood. At the same time the intellectual currents were running against the church. Deism, the rationalistic faith which had swept through England, now became the religion of many American leaders. Despite the heroic efforts of the Princeton faculty, most of the students in the college were professed deists or complete agnostics. The answer of the Prsebyterian Church to this state of affairs was to insist on ever more stringent academic qualifications for their clergy. To combat the heterodoxy of the deists, the church placed increased emphasis on doctrinal conformity and a rigid orthodoxy. The frontier settlements of Pennsylvania, Maryland, Virginia, and farther west were, at the same time, crying for more ministers. Their need was not so much for learned experts in dogmatic theology as for warm-hearted, hard-working pastors. Several attempts were made to lower the educational requirements for the Presbyterian clergy, but each time Witherspoon and his friends beat them down. The result was to turn over most of the opportunities on the frontier to the Methodists and Baptists, but at the same time to retain leadership in the larger urban areas and in the realm of public affairs and original thinking.* Unlike the Methodists, the Presbyterians had devised a thor-

* Leonard J. Trinterud, *The Forming of an American Tradition* (Philadelphia, 1949), 266-268.

83

oughly democratic manner for calling a minister and for carrying out the business of the church, but the high level of education among the clergy necessarily gave them a place of prominence over the laity.

To provide the necessary education, presbyteries were urged to establish parochial schools in their bounds to create a literate constituency. Not many actually complied, though the New Brunswick presbytery made several attempts. Princeton College, meanwhile, recovered slowly from the losses of the war years, though it soon became evident that it could not train ministers in the necessary theological disciplines at the same time that it maintained a superior curriculum in liberal arts. It was for this reason that the General Assembly, after much debate, decided to establish a Theological Seminary adjacent to Princeton College. Within a few years of its founding in 1812 it became one of the most notable institutions of its kind in the country, and during much of the nineteenth century it provided a preponderant share of the leadership in the Presbyterian Church.*

By 1835 the religious climate in New Jersey had begun to improve. The tides of infidelity which rose to a peak during the French Revolution and which left their mark on the churches, began to recede. From the low mark in 1800 when less than 8 per cent of all Americans were members of any church body, the figure slowly rose. There were many discouragements yet to be faced, but the universal condition of weakness in which all the churches found themselves had one happy result. Some of the bitterness among denominations began to melt away as they faced the vast forces of irreligion around them. So much remained to be done and so limited were the resources to do it that no church could afford to waste itself on denominational hostilities. For this insight, their children of a later day could be grateful.

* Nelson R. Burr, *Education in New Jersey, 1630-1871* (Princeton, 1942), Chapter VIII.

IV

STORM CLOUDS ACROSS
THE CHURCH
1835-1870

THE MIDDLE DECADES of the nineteenth century confronted the religious bodies of New Jersey with two
highly significant issues: expansion and slavery. By this
time, of course, New Jersey was no longer regarded as
being on the frontier. Like the other original colonies
along the seacoast, it now enjoyed the advantages of
urban life, of fairly easy communications, and a stable
society. Most of the inhabitants regarded themselves as
sophisticated "Easterners" quite unlike the crude frontiersmen of Ohio, Kentucky, and points west. Jerseymen
had plenty of problems, to be sure: inflation, economic
dependence on Philadelphia and New York, loss of some
of their best citizens in the westward migration, etc. But
their problems were quite different from those experienced
by settlers on the frontier. It was easy and natural for the
seaboard states to take a parochial view of religion as
most of them did of politics and economics. There were
so many problems confronting the church at home that
it was a great temptation to let the frontier fend for
itself. Those churches which did so, however, found their
internal growth hampered so that their problems were
eventually compounded.

Among them was the Dutch Reformed Church, whose New Jersey congregations were preoccupied with recovering from the devastation caused by the Revolution. It was not unconcern with the frontier as such which caused their lack of interest but the fact that very few of the frontiersmen were Dutch. Clinging tenaciously to their national heritage, they largely restricted their services to those of Dutch descent. This was true long after their worship was conducted in English and the close contact with the Netherlands had been broken. Whenever opportunity arose to serve Dutch frontiersmen, the New Jersey Reformed congregations willingly responded, as happened in 1846. A group of colonists from the Netherlands stopped in New York on the way to Michigan and were befriended by the Dutch Reformed congregations along the way.* In the years that followed offerings for the western settlers were taken up in New Jersey churches. In addition the interest in foreign missions secured support from the Dutch as early as it did among any other church body in the State. Yet the denomination failed to grow very significantly, its strength in New Jersey being concentrated in the area north of the Raritan. Not until 1867 was the official name of the denomination changed from the Reformed Protestant Dutch Church to the Reformed Church in America,** long after the other churches in the State had become thoroughly Americanized.

Another communion that shared many of the same difficulties as the Dutch were the Lutherans. Their constituents were chiefly German, and for a long time there was strong resistance to introducing the English language into their worship services. Since the German immigrants

* Edward T. Corwin, *Manual of the Reformed Church in America* (4th ed.; New York, 1902), 138.
** *Acts and Proceedings of the Sixty First General Synod of the Reformed Protestant Dutch Church in North America, 1867,* Appendix.

settled at first around Philadelphia and to a lesser extent around New York City, these became important Lutheran centers. The number of Lutheran churches in New Jersey, on the other hand, remained small. In addition to the language problem, the Jersey Lutherans were divided between the Philadelphia and New York factions which disagreed sharply with each other on a number of issues. The New York churches were fairly liberal in their theological outlook, were affected by the rationalism of the time, adopted English quite early, and tended to favor merger with the Episcopalians. Those in Philadelphia, on the other hand, were militantly orthodox in their theology and quite conservative in outlook. They resisted the use of English and began exploring the possibilities of union with the German Reformed churches about them.* Caught in the middle, the New Jersey Lutherans gravitated toward the center nearest them, or they abandoned their church and joined another. The end result was to keep Lutheranism weak in the State.

SCHISM AMONG FRIENDS

The Society of Friends was still another body which suffered from internal dissension and thus failed to appeal to any who were not already Friends by birthright. By nature undemonstrative, the Quakers of the early nineteenth century made little attempt to evangelize those about them or proselyte for their faith. In New Jersey they were concentrated around Philadelphia and along the Delaware up to Trenton, with a few scattered meetings elsewhere in the state. Thanks to the discipline of their elders they were able to maintain a fairly constant number but without much growth. The man who changed this condition was a Quaker preacher from Long Island named Elias Hicks who plunged the Society into a bitter controversy which ultimately led to schism. The issues were originally doctrinal but finally revolved

* Abdel R. Wentz, *A Basic History of Lutheranism in America* (Philadelphia, 1955), 74-77.

around freedom of conscience.* Hicks was a liberal. His dependence on the Inner Light led him to regard all else, including the Scriptures and even Christ himself, as subsidiary and not entirely necessary. This teaching scandalized the orthodox Quakers of Philadelphia, who accepted the authority of the Scriptures and the doctrine of Christ's atonement as essential. The two views finally clashed head-on in the Philadelphia Yearly Meeting with much recrimination on both sides. Unfortunately, neither group was able to understand the other. To Hicks, who embodied some of the liberal spirit of the times, each person should be given considerable latitude in determining his own doctrinal position. The Inner Light directs different people in different ways, and therefore all Christians, and especially Quakers, should avoid authoritarianism and allow a wide diversity of opinion with regard to dogma. The Philadelphia elders were vociferous in their disagreement. Fearful that such easy tolerance would lead to divisions and a loss of unity, they insisted that doctrine was absolutely essential. One can almost hear the shade of George Keith wryly muttering, "I told you so!"

The issue finally came to a head in 1827 at the Yearly Meeting in Philadelphia. Even though Hicks' doctrinal views were not widely attractive, his views on liberty of conscience were. Many Friends resented the way the "overseers and clerks" in Philadelphia ran the meetings almost as if they were a private domain. Country Friends grumbled that the city leaders, who guarded the copies of the Discipline, kept them "as secret and sacred as the books of the Hindoos." ** They also complained that the Philadelphia Friends, many of whom were men of wealth and culture, had abandoned the ideal of simplicity in

* Bliss Forbush, *Elias Hicks: Quaker Liberal* (New York, 1956), Chapters 17, 18.
** Quoted in A. C. Thomas and R. H. Thomas, *History of the Society of Friends in America;* Vol. XII of the "American Church History Series" (New York, 1894), 257.

living characteristic of their founding fathers. Hicks was a Long Island farmer as well as a preacher, and the "common people heard him gladly." The upshot was a split in the Society.* Taking as their rallying cry, "God alone is Lord of the conscience," the Hicksites organized Monthly and Yearly Meetings of their own. For a long time there was an unseemly battle in the New Jersey courts over the control of Society property which was only settled when the New Jersey State Legislature passed a bill providing for a division of the property. More than half of the New Jersey Friends adhered to the Hicksite camp, and the divisions and litigation which ensued weakened the Quaker witness in south Jersey. Once again the tension between New York and Philadelphia had disrupted the life of one of New Jersey's religious bodies. Nor was this the last time such a division would occur.

In 1837, America was visited by the brilliant convert to Quakerism, Joseph J. Gurney of Earlham Hall. Well-educated and highly articulate, Gurney had tried in his writings to reconcile the mystical concept of the Inner Light with a well-ordered theology and intellectual discipline. The Philadelphia Quakers were charmed by his manners and simplicity in spite of his wealth and learning. During his frequent trips between New York and Philadelphia, Gurney was able to visit a large number of Hicksite Friends in New Jersey, and he repeatedly expressed his sorrow over the schism in the Quaker fellowship. It was his intention to serve as a mediating influence between the Orthodox and Hicksite groups. Unhappily, his efforts merely resulted in another split, when a New England Quaker named John Wilbur undertook a violent attack on Gurney. The upshot was that the Orthodox Friends in New Jersey were divided between the two camps after Wilbur was censured by his own Yearly Meeting in 1845. Thereafter there were three bodies of Friends in the State: Wilburite, Gurneyite, and Hicksite, a fact

* For a trenchant analysis of the causes, see Elbert Russell, *The History of Quakerism* (New York, 1942), Chapter 22.

which helps explain the decline of Quaker growth and influence.*

In contrast to the internal dissensions among the Lutherans and Quakers, the New Jersey Diocese of the Episcopalian Church made history of another sort. When Bishop Croes died in 1832 there were but 18 Episcopal priests in the State serving 27 parishes. By 1859 the diocesan records show 98 priests and 85 parishes while communicant membership grew in the same period from 900 to 5000.** Much of the credit for this remarkable achievement must be given to the second Episcopal bishop in New Jersey, George Washington Doane. Few men have combined such varied and seemingly contradictory gifts as did Bishop Doane. While he was a High Churchman who regarded the Tractarian movement in England † with warm approval, he was also an evangelical preacher with a deep concern for converting the unchurched. He was a sensitive poet and hymn writer, but also a builder of schools and churches. His concern for liturgy and sacraments led to weekly communion and the celebration of saints' days in the church. But at the same time he was committed to the missionary outreach of the church, not only in his diocese, but to the ends of the earth. Born in Trenton, the son of a carpenter and contractor, he received his education in New York where he fell under the influence of Bishop John Henry Hobart, the epitome of High Churchmanship. He also became an excellent

---

* See *Memoirs of Joseph John Gurney* (Philadelphia, 1854), II, 125, 132. Also see David E. Swift, *Joseph John Gurney* (Middletown, 1962), 189 f.

** Nelson R. Burr, *The Anglican Church in New Jersey* (Philadelphia, 1954), 463.

† A movement begun by a series of tracts written by Oxford churchmen. It emphasized liturgy, a high view of the sacraments, and closer relations with the Roman Catholic Church.

scholar and writer. These abilities proved useful when he became embroiled with controversial issues, as he so often was.

It was while he was serving as Rector of Trinity Church in Boston, that he was elected to the episcopate and also became Rector of St. Mary's Church, Burlington. From then on he was engaged in a vigorous campaign to strengthen his diocese. He traveled a great deal, organizing new parishes, confirming parishioners, and securing new candidates for the priesthood. The results were heartening. Within ten years the diocese more than doubled the size of its membership and churches. More important, the church was united as it had never been before. Two important emphases of the Bishop contributed to this. On the one hand he enriched the worship of his church by introducing some of the hymnody of the Oxford Movement to the New Jersey communicants and he vigorously defended the High Church view of worship against the accusations of popery which were leveled against him.* In the second place, he awakened the church to its missionary task. He was a leader in getting the General Convention to create the office of missionary bishop, and he preached the sermon at the consecration of the first one to be sent out. On that occasion, he said,

Brethren, the field is the whole world. To every soul of man, in every part of it, the Gospel is to be preached. Everywhere, the Gospel is to be preached *by, through,* and in the Church. . . . Professing these things, act accordingly.**

In his own parish he inaugurated the weekly-envelope system of giving to missions and he edited a missionary paper. Little wonder, then, that the church grew steadily under his leadership, and at his death a hymn which he wrote suggested an appropriate epitaph:

* George W. Doane, *Life and Writings* (New York, 1860), I, 402 ff.
** Preached at the Consecration of the Reverend Jackson Kemper, D.D., Sept. 25, 1835, George W. Doane, *Life and Writings* (New York, 1860), II, 413.

Softly now the light of day
Fades upon my sight away;
Free from care, from labour free,
Lord, I would commune with Thee.*

METHODISM ON THE MARCH

The same steady growth was also found among New Jersey Methodists. Though it was on the western frontier that Methodism scored its most dramatic successes, the organization which worked so well there proved equally effective in New Jersey. The secret of the Methodist system lay in its mobility. The circuit riders or itinerant ministry traveled ceaselessly around the circuit of small churches or classes, preaching, teaching, and co-ordinating the work of the local leadership. This local ministry, which was usually unordained, consisted of the class leaders, the exhorters, and the local preachers. Such instruction as they received had to come from books and from the guidance of the traveling preachers, who after a probationary period were ordained as deacons and then as elders. Most of the traveling preachers were recruited from the ranks of the local preachers. When a young man showed some promise in preaching and felt called to give full time to it, he was appointed to a circuit and given a certain number of books to master in preparation for ordination. Frequently he was associated with a more experienced man on a larger circuit, so that he learned from observation as well as experience. When a probationer was considered ready by the conference bishop, he would be ordained by the Quarterly Conference of which he was a member. The circuit riders, however, were not only to visit organized societies, but to establish new ones as well. The Methodist *Discipline* made this clear:

You have nothing to do but to save souls. Therefore spend and be spent in this work. And go always not only to those that want, but to those that want you most. Observe. It is not your

* George W. Doane, "Songs by the Way," in *Life and Writings* (New York, 1860), I, 9.

business to preach so many times, and to take care of this or that society only: But to save as many souls as you can; to bring as many sinners as you possibly can to repentance, and with all your power to build them up in that holiness, without which they cannot see the Lord.*

No man in New Jersey took these words more seriously during the early nineteenth century than Charles Pitman, the Methodist preacher and missionary. Born near Cookstown in Burlington County just after the Revolutionary War, he felt called early in life to follow the vocation of minister in the Methodist Church. He served as exhorter and local preacher in his home church and then was appointed as itinerant preacher to the Trenton circuit in 1817 when he was twenty-one years of age. At that time the circuit covered nine preaching stations in an area bounded by Crosswicks, Hightstown, Princeton, and Pennington. It meant a great deal of time on horseback, but he had a boundless enthusiasm for his work which attracted new converts. At this time the Methodists were not regarded very highly, but public opinion of them seems to have gone up wherever Pitman carried on his ministry. When Pitman was appointed to New Brunswick, there were but 17 members on the roll of the Methodist Society there. It was not long, however, until the congregation began to grow, attracted by the preaching and even more by the singing of the ardent young minister. Like Asbury and the other early Methodist preachers, Pitman was at heart an evangelist and missionary. Recognizing his talents, the Methodist Bishop appointed Pitman as Presiding Elder of West New Jersey, which comprised most of the southern counties of the State, and later made him Presiding Elder of East New Jersey.**

* "Form of Discipline for the Ministers, Preachers, and Members of the Methodist Episcopal Church in America, 1787," quoted in Smith, Handy and Loetscher, *American Christianity* (New York, 1960), I, 458. See William W. Sweet, *Religion on the American Frontier:* Volume IV, *The Methodists* (Chicago, 1946), 42-50.

** C. A. Malmsbury, *The Life, Labors and Sermons of Rev. Charles Pitman, D. D.* (Philadelphia, 1887), 35-79.

Methodist services in those days were lively experiences for all who took part. One preaching station near Freehold got the name "Screaming Hill" because of the exuberant emotionalism of the worship there. The great enemy of religion, as the Methodists saw it, was formalism, the emphasis on external rites at the expense of inner experience. Christianity, they insisted, was nothing if it was not experienced in the heart. Orthodoxy was no substitute for conversion. So while the Presbyterians and Anglicans emphasized doctrine and liturgy in their worship, the Methodists preached for conversion, using every emotional device they knew. Pitman was a master at this kind of appeal, and churches began to spring up in south Jersey where there had been no churches before. A congregation was gathered in this way outside Cape May. They had much enthusiasm but little cash, so they did not know how they were going to raise funds to build a church. Whereupon Pitman preached long and earnestly to secure funds for the building. At length a recent convert came forward saying, "The Lord has blessed my soul and I thank Him for it. I have no money, but I have a flock of fine sheep, and you may have the whole flock." *

For many years thereafter the Methodist Church in Cape May was known as the product of Mr. Pitman's "sheep sermon." In later life Pitman was appointed Corresponding Secretary of the Missionary Society of the Methodist Episcopal Church. It would have been difficult to find a more appropriate man for that position, since he had been a missionary all his life. Most of the Methodist churches erected in New Jersey between 1825 and 1850 owed their founding to the work of Charles Pitman and the preachers under his care.

With this kind of vigorous leadership, it is little wonder that Methodist congregations sprang up wherever a small village or a few farm families were located. By 1836 the number of circuits in New Jersey was too great

* C. A. Malmsbury, *The Life, Labors and Sermons of Rev. Charles Pitman, D.D.* (Philadelphia, 1887), 59.

for the Philadelphia Conference to administer efficiently so the New Jersey Conference was created to cover all the Methodist churches in New Jersey and also a few in New York. Twenty years later a further subdivision was made creating the New Jersey Conference in the southern part of the State and the Newark Conference in the north.* In addition to planting new churches throughout the State, New Jersey Methodists also had a significant role in providing funds for opening new circuits on the western frontier and also sent a number of their sons to be itinerant preachers there. Learner Blackman, who came from Bargaintown near Somers Point in south Jersey, served as a missionary in the Ohio River valley. Judson S. Hill, from Trenton, went to Tennessee and established a school for Negroes near Morristown, Tennessee while William Roberts, who was born in Burlington, traveled to the West Coast and built the first Methodist church in San Francisco.**

OLD AND NEW SCHOOL PRESBYTERIANS

Predictably, the Presbyterians were deeply embroiled in controversy during most of the first half of the nineteenth century, and the New Jersey members were involved in more than their share. The root of the difficulty lay in a common-sense agreement worked out between the New England Congregationalists and the Presbyterians of the Middle Atlantic States. The agreement, known as the Plan of Union of 1801, provided that each church would refrain from trespassing on the territory of the other (one reason why Congregational churches were late in coming to New Jersey) and also set up a scheme for jointly supplying the unchurched areas of western New York, northern Ohio, and Illinois. Any congregation in these areas from either church could call a minister from either church. Thus a Congregational church could call a Pres-

* *Journal of the General Conference, 1856,* 283.
** Frank B. Stanger, *The Methodist Trail in New Jersey* (Camden, 1961), 51 f.

byterian minister and vice versa. As it turned out, not many Congregational clergy left New England, so most of the churches in the area covered by the Plan of Union eventually called Presbyterian ministers, and in the course of time they b.ecame Presbyterian congregations.

At first glance, this situation appeared to be wholly favorable to the Presbyterians. It is true that they gained a number of churches, but they did so at the cost of uniformity. Congregational practices began to creep into the Church. Even more serious, the liberal theologies of the New England schools such as Hopkinsianism, the New Haven theology, and Finney revivalism, got a strong foothold in these "Presbygational" churches. Worse, some of the adherents of these doctrines settled in New Jersey, the seat of Calvinistic orthodoxy. Albert Barnes, pastor of the Presbyterian Church in Morristown was an outstanding example. Although a graduate of Princeton Theological Seminary, he showed some of the traits of Methodism in his preaching, a fact explained by his membership in the Methodist Church up to the time he entered the seminary. While still at Morristown, Barnes published a sermon entitled, "The Way of Salvation," and shortly afterward he was called to the pastorate of the First Presbyterian Church of Philadelphia, perhaps the most prestigious congregation in the whole church. Meanwhile, the sermon came to the attention of Dr. Ashbel Green, President of the Board of Directors of Princeton Seminary, editor of the *Christian Advocate,* and self-appointed watchdog of orthodoxy. His critical eye pounced on a number of statements which agreed with the New Haven theology and directly contradicted the Westminister Confession, and so he tried to block Barnes' call to Philadelphia. This proved to be but the opening gun in a struggle between the Old School party, led by Green, and the New School, represented by Barnes and those who found fault with the strict Calvinism of the Confession. Eventually Barnes was acquitted by the General Assembly, but not before the orthodoxy of many of the New York presbyteries and of the newly-established

Lane Seminary in Cincinnati had been called into question.

In 1836 the New School party founded Union Theological Seminary in New York City which immediately provided a center for liberal churchmen. Princeton Seminary, meanwhile, continued to be the rallying ground for the Old School conservatives. The following year, the General Assembly meeting in Philadelphia abrogated the Plan of Union of 1801, and proceeded to eject from the church the four northeastern synods which had been created under that Plan. It was no small expulsion, since the offending synods constituted nearly one-half the membership of the undivided church. The schism thus created was to last until after the Civil War.* There were many on both sides who regretted the precipitate action of the Assembly and who questioned whether such a drastic course was really necessary. In part it was the result of the Presbyterian insistence on a highly trained ministry. Schooled in theological debate their clergy was unusually sensitive to theological subtleties of all kinds and so tended to make doctrinal orthodoxy essential to salvation.**

SLAVERY: THE INESCAPABLE ISSUE

It is possible that there was another cause for the split. Even though slavery was not mentioned in the Assembly debates, this was an issue that had already begun to stir up the North and to create resentment in the South. According to at least one authority, the absence of reference to it can be explained only by the fact that the

* For details of the schism see E. H. Gillett, *History of the Presbyterian Church* (Philadelphia, 1864), II; Samuel J. Baird, *A History of the New School* (Philadelphia, 1868); and William W. Sweet, *Religion on the American Frontier:* Volume II *The Presbyterians* (New York, 1936).

** See Isaac V. Brown, *A Historical Vindication of the Abrogation of the Plan of Union by the Presbyterian Church* (Philadelphia, 1855); and Zebulon Crocker, *The Catastrophe of the Presbyterian Church in 1837* (New Haven, 1838).

conservative faction needed southern votes to drive out the northern liberals from the church.* Certainly from this time on slavery increasingly became the unavoidable topic in American life, and since it was widely regarded as a moral issue the churches were drawn inevitably into the debate. New Jersey was especially sensitive because of its geographical location and the variety of its religious bodies. As a New Jersey Congressman put it in a speech before the House of Representatives:

I am not precisely certain whether I should class the State from which I come among the Northern, or Southern States. If that magic line, of which we hear so much, known as Mason and Dixon's line, should run through to the Atlantic, it will cut our State directly in two, leaving part of it on each side of the line. And besides this, I find, on looking at the map, that the southerly part of the State of New Jersey is on the same parallel with the District of Columbia, which with that part of the State of Maryland lying north of it, claims, I believe, to be purely southern; but whether it be southern, northern, or neither, one thing is pretty certain, that neither she nor any of her representatives are very fanatical on the subject of slavery.**

The reason, quite simply, was that slavery was almost extinct in New Jersey by that time. This had not always been the case. Prior to the Revolution slaves had been fairly plentiful in New Jersey. Indeed, from 1737 to 1800 the number of slaves increased every year until they numbered 12,422. Most of the slaveowners appear to have been Dutch or German farmers, though slaves were common as domestic servants as well. In 1776 there was only one home in Perth Amboy served by free white domestics.† Many of the rest who had domestics presumably used slave labor.

* William W. Sweet, *Religion on the American Frontier:* Volume II, *The Presbyterians* (New York, 1936), 122 ff.
** *Speech of Mr. John Van Dyke, of New Jersey, Delivered in the House of Representatives, Mar. 4, 1850* (Washington, 1850), 4.
† William A. Whitehead, *Contributions to the Early History of Perth Amboy* (New York, 1856), 317.

What changed this condition was a growing feeling on the part of the people that slavery was wrong, and this was reflected in a series of legislative acts designed to restrict and finally to abolish slavery altogether. In 1786 the New Jersey State Legislature passed an act forbidding the further importation of slaves into the State. This was succeeded by "An Act for the Gradual Abolition of Slavery" in 1804.* It was not until 1846 that slavery was abolished by statute, though it merely provided that all existing slaves would thereafter be known as apprentices. One advantage, however, was that no apprentice could be sold without his consent in writing, and, as a result, the number of slaves in the State declined to 674 in 1840; and by 1860 there were only 18 "apprentices" left.** Among the religious bodies which contributed to the changing climate of opinion, the Society of Friends played an outstanding role. The spirit of John Woolman was still very much alive as evidenced in the certificate of manumission issued by Moore Furman in 1784:

I, Moore Furman, being convinced of the iniquity and in-humanity of slavery and desirous of discouraging the same have manumitted my negroman slave, Thomas . . .†

The Society to Promote the Abolition of Slavery was formed in New Jersey as early as 1786, which worked to abolish slavery through legislation, with what success we have already seen. It was never a very large group, but it was influential. In 1824 the Friends published a small pamphlet which documented from letters and interviews the nefarious character of the slave trade. The purpose

* A. Q. Keasby, "Slavery in New Jersey," *Proceedings of The New Jersey Historical Society*, IV, No. 3, 147-154.
** Henry S. Cooley, *A Study of Slavery in New Jersey* (Baltimore, 1896), 31, 46 f.; D. H. Gardner, "The Emancipation of Slaves in New Jersey," *Proceedings of The New Jersey Historical Society*, New Series, IX, No. 1, 1-21.
† Quoted by Hubert Schmidt, "Slavery and Attitudes on Slavery, Hunterdon County, N. J.," *Proceedings of The New Jersey Historical Society*, LVIII, No. 4, 240.

of the tract, "A View of the Present State of the African Slave Trade," was apparently to arouse public opinion against slavery.

It was a Presbyterian, the Reverend Doctor Robert Finley, who led in the attempt to solve the slavery problem by establishing a colony for slaves in Africa. He was pastor of the Presbyterian Church of Basking Ridge (at that time called Baskenridge) and headmaster of the Basking Ridge Academy when he thought of the colonization plan as a practical solution to slavery. Going to Washington he interviewed President Monroe and leaders of Congress who at first were skeptical about the whole venture. Finally, Henry Clay gave his support, and the American Colonization Society came into being in 1816. Later Finley helped organize a state branch which was active off and on until the 1840's. Support for it came chiefly from churches in the Newark area, notably Presbyterian and Dutch Reformed.* Meanwhile, more radical voices were being heard in the north. In New York the American and Foreign Anti-Slavery Society charged that "American Slavery is at war with the Declaration of Independence, the Constitution of the United States, natural justice, and Christianity" and, "Slavery is a sin against God and a crime against man." ** The southern slave-owner was portrayed in the blackest terms, while the condition of his wretched Negroes was described in such a way as to arouse both pity and anger. A hymnal was even published by the American Anti-Slavery Society which contained such lachrymose offerings as:

> Mother! whene'er, around your child,
> You clasp your arms in love,
> And when, with grateful joy, you raise
> Your eyes to God above;—

* See *Historical Notes on Slavery and Colonization*, etc. (Elizabeth-Town, 1842).
** *Thirteenth Annual Report of the American and Foreign Anti-Slavery Society*, as quoted by Samuel B. How, *Slaveholding Not Sinful* (New York, 1855), 7, 8.

Think of the wretched mother, when
Her child is torn away,
Sold for a slave; and will you not
For that poor mother pray?

or, from the same collection, to a more martial air:

Strike off my galling fetters, strike!
My shackles rend in twain.
Unloose the yoke from off my neck,
And break my heavy chain;
Oh! let the breath of liberty
My burning temples fan;
For has not God created me,
A *brother* and a *man?* *

With such extravagant sentiments, however, most Jersey churchmen were not in sympathy. Few ministers had much to say on slavery in their sermons until the late fifties, and those who did were apt to face criticism from their parishioners. In the 1840's Robert Landis was forced to leave the pastorate of the Presbyterian Church of Bethlehem, N. J. because of his inveterate hostility to slavery.** But most ministers were like the Reverend J. G. Williamson, a later pastor in the same church, who was able to remain in his pulpit unchallenged for over fifty years because even though he is said to have opposed slavery, in the pulpit he "stayed off worldly topics and stuck to sermons about Christ and him crucified." † The justification for this silence usually was that slavery was too closely identified with politics to be treated from the pulpit. Even after war broke out, a Presbyterian minister in Philadelphia stated:

* Edwin F. Hatfield (ed.), *Freedom's Lyre* (New York, 1840), Nos. 111 and 33.
** Robert W. Landis, *Bethlehem Church and its Pastor* (Printed for the author, 1851), 13.
† Hubert Schmidt, "Slavery and Attitudes Toward Slavery, Hunterdon County, N. J.," *Proceedings of The New Jersey Historical Society*, LVIII, No. 4, 244.

When the pulpit meddles with party politics, it becomes an engine of mischief. But it may and must enforce upon the people the duty of carrying into their politics the truthfulness, the integrity, and the charity, to which they are bound in every other sphere.*

Yet not all were silent. In keeping with the strong anti-slavery resolution voiced by their denominational Assembly, the New Jersey Presbyterians as early as 1818 had adopted in their Synod a pronouncement: "It is the duty of all Christians to use their honest, earnest, and unwearied endeavors . . . to obtain the complete abolition of slavery." ** This was before the abolitionists became violent and before the New School–Old School split in the Presbyterian Church. From 1838 on, however, the Old School Presbyterians increasingly hedged. Writing in the *Biblical Repertory and Princeton Review* for 1838, Charles Hodge cautioned:

The mass of the pious and thinking people in this country are neither abolitionists nor the advocates of slavery. They stand where they have ever stood on the broad scriptural foundation; maintaining the obligation of all men in their several places and relations, to act on the law of love, and to promote the spiritual and temporal welfare of others by every means in their power.

He then went on to attack abolitionism and to assert that slaveholding is not necessarily sinful. Since slaveholders had been welcomed in the Early Church, Christians could not consistently eject them from the Church now. The answer to slaveholding was not anti-slavery legislation or violent abolitionist propaganda, but gradual emancipation, with remuneration to their masters, and possibly mass resettlement in Africa.†

* Henry Boardman, *The Peace We Need and How to Secure It* (Philadelphia, 1865), 23.
** Hubert Schmidt, "Slavery and Attitudes Toward Slavery, Hunterdon County, N. J.," *Proceedings of The New Jersey Historical Society*, LVIII, No. 4, 243.
† *Biblical Repertory and Princeton Review*, XVI (1844), 545 ff.

A similar line was taken by some members of the Dutch Reformed Church. In 1855 a delegation from the German Reformed Classis of North Carolina approached the General Synod of the Dutch Reformed Church suggesting a union of the two bodies. After some debate the Synod voted to lay the matter on the table because such a union would endanger the peace of the church and "expose it to being distracted by the agitation of the question of slavery" especially since, in the mind of the Synod, "slavery is sinful." Among the delegates to the Synod was Samuel B. How, Pastor of the First Reformed Church of New Brunswick. As soon as he reached home he wrote an angry retort entitled, "Slaveholding Not Sinful," which attacked on scriptural grounds, the presuppositions of the abolitionists. It should be noted that neither How, nor the other conservatives of New Jersey, defended slavery as good. Rather, it was "one of the penal effects of the fall, and of the great wickedness of men." *
At the same time, it was not sufficiently serious to deprive a slaveholder of church membership. This position was grounded in the exegesis of relevant biblical passages such as Paul's discussion of slavery (I Tim. 6:1-5; Philemon) and Christ's comments on slavery (e.g., the healing of the centurion's slave, Luke 7:2-10) . Since the Bible did not condemn slavery per se, then Christians are not warranted in doing so.

No sooner did Dr. How's article appear than it, too, was attacked. John Van Dyke, a New Jersey Representative in Congress, took the good pastor to task for defending "the blackest, foulest, and most disgraceful stain which rests on the country of which we are so justly proud, and which we love so well." ** Without attempting to examine specific texts, Van Dyke, like those who denounced

* Samuel B. How, *Slaveholding Not Sinful* (New York, 1855), 29. See *Acts and Proceedings of the General Synod of the Reformed Protestant Dutch Church*, VIII (1849-1855), 531-532, and IX (1855-1860), 12-14.
** John Van Dyke, *Slaveholding Not Sinful: A Reply to the Argument of Dr. How* (New Brunswick, 1856), 3.

slavery outright, charged it with being opposed to the overall spirit of the Scriptures as well as being irreconcilable with Christian morality.

Most churchmen in New Jersey, so far as they had any convictions one way or another, were against slavery, but they were equally against violence. The Methodists, Baptists, Friends, and New School Presbyterians were most vocal in their anti-slavery stand, while the Episcopalians, Dutch Reformed, and Old School Presbyterians were moderate or neutral.* Meanwhile, tensions within the national denominations built up to the breaking point. By 1840 there were already strong voices in the Methodist Church denouncing slavery, but the General Conference refused to permit a discussion of the subject fearing that to do so would split the church. Unsatisfied with this craven solution, a number of the anti-slavery leaders seceded in 1843 to form the Wesleyan Methodist Church, though very few from New Jersey were involved in the new movement.

Much closer to home was the Baptist split in 1845 which led to the formation of the Southern Baptist Convention. The few Baptist churches in New Jersey remained with the northern branch of the denomination, but the split seriously weakened the church. All the Baptist pastors in the State were either neutral toward slavery or opposed it. There was none who defended slavery as a positive good, but very few were champions of abolition, either. The most outstanding Baptist minister who was an abolitionist, Samuel Aaron of Burlington, tried to get the Baptist State Convention to go on record against

* See John H. Hopkins, Episcopal Bishop of Vermont, *A Scriptural, Ecclesiastical, and Historical View of Slavery* (New York, 1864) and reply by Reverend J. B. Dobbins, Pastor of Methodist Episcopal Church of Camden, *The Bible Against Slavery* (Philadelphia, 1864). For an Episcopal sermon see Benjamin Dorr, Rector of Christ Church, Philadelphia, *The American Vine* (Philadelphia, 1861) and an Old School Presbyterian, Samuel J. Baird of Woodbury, *Southern Rights and Northern Duties* (Philadelphia, 1861).

slavery, but he was voted down by his colleagues who wanted to keep the subject out of public debate.*

The Methodist Episcopal Church was the next to face the question, after .a bitter debate over a slaveholding bishop. In 1845 the southern conferences of the Methodist church withdrew to form the Methodist Episcopal Church, South. The withdrawal left the northern half of the church free to engage in open anti-slavery agitation, and very soon it numbered in its membership the strongest advocates of abolition.

The Presbyterians were able to stay united longer. Since the vast majority of the New School Presbyterians were in the North, they came out strongly for abolition. As a result the few New School congregations in the South withdrew in 1857 to form the United Synod of the Presbyterian Church. The Old School branch, however, with its strong conservative tone refused to take a stand on slavery right up to the Civil War. The majority opinion appeared to be that slavery, while a regrettable evil, was not necessarily sinful. When Fort Sumter was fired on, a new element entered into the debate. The General Assembly met in Philadelphia a few weeks later, and almost at once a northern delegate moved to give some expression of devotion to the Federal Union. At first the motion was tabled, but so great was the pressure from the northern delegates that eventually it was taken up and passed. The conservatism of the North could live with slavery but not with rebellion! This, of course, was totally unacceptable to the South, so the southern half seceded to form the Presbyterian Church in the Confederate States of America a few months later.

Almost the only major Protestant denomination not split by the Civil War was the Episcopal Church. Though the southern branch had organized a Protestant Episcopal Church in the Confederate States of America, this

* Norman Maring, *A History of New Jersey Baptists* (Unpublished MS held by New Jersey Baptist Convention, East Orange), Chapter V, 22-24.

split was never recognized by the Triennial Convention, and since that body had consistently refused to make pronouncements on any issue that was remotely political, there was little to offend either branch of the Church. Consequently, as soon as the Civil War ended, the southern delegates took their seats in the next Triennial Convention without question.

The outbreak of war ended most of the debate over slavery in New Jersey. The issue now was secession and rebellion. Even such a staunch conservative as Charles Hodge, who defended slavery on biblical grounds right up to the end, gave his support to the Union and the war effort, because the South, in his opinion, had no legitimate right to secede.* Presbyterians, Methodists, and Dutch Reformed pastors united to denounce the South for disrupting the Union and inaugurating the war, while little was said about slavery.** More astonishing was the willingness of some pastors to assume part of the guilt for the causes of the war. Dr. Roswell Hitchcock, a professor at Union Seminary in New York declaimed, "Let no one section of our common country angrily upbraid another for its vices or its crimes. We are all offenders, all of us, North and South, East and West." †

CHURCHES IN THE WAR

The young men, meanwhile, marched off to war, and some within the churches became concerned about their Christian nurture. The idea of having clergymen join the army as chaplains already had a long tradition behind it, so naturally this was the first approach. There was no

* See "The Princeton Review on the State of the Country and the Church," *Biblical Repertory and Princeton Review,* XXXVII (1865), 637 f.

** Cf. I. N. Sprague, *The Duty of Sustaining the Government* (Newark, 1861); James Neill, *Reasons for our Opposition to the Southern Confederacy* (Philadelphia, 1861); J. W. Jackson, *The Sentiments and Conduct Proper to the Present Crisis in our National Affairs* (Philadelphia, 1861).

† Roswell D. Hitchcock, *Our National Sin* (New York, 1861), 23.

lack of volunteers at the beginning but the program as a whole had indifferent success. For one thing, the appointment of chaplains was a regimental responsibility left up to the regimental commander who got the vote of his company commanders and field officers before making the appointment. The regimental commanders who did not wish to be bothered by a chaplain simply made no appointment. Further, the pay of "Captain of Cavalry" which was originally stipulated for chaplains was repeatedly cut, and unlike the other officers, they had to pay for their food, board, and travel out of their own pockets. It is not surprising, then, to find that as the war progressed resignations were frequent and volunteers few. The President of the United States was authorized by law to appoint chaplains to hospitals wherever the need was indicated. But the appointments were never sufficient to the need, so many regimental chaplains were drawn off for hospital duty. Since there was no Chief of Chaplains or Chaplain's Division to give guidance and support, individual chaplains were largely left to their own devices in planning a program and securing religious supplies. Not surprisingly there were frequent complaints that the chaplains were ineffective or even a hindrance.* All told, there were 47 chaplains reported as serving with New Jersey regiments throughout the war, one of whom died of wounds received in action: Chaplain Francis E. Butler of the Twenty-fifth Regiment was shot while carrying water to some wounded men during the seige at Suffolk, Virginia.**

More effective, perhaps, in meeting the religious needs of the men at the front, was the United States Christian Commission. This was a civilian agency set up by the Young Men's Christian Association to deal specifically with the needs of the armed forces during the war. The

* "Religious Instruction in the Army," *The Biblical Repertory and Princeton Review*, XXXV (1863), 383-403.
** H. Clay Trumbull, *War Memories of an Army Chaplain* (New York, 1898), 10. See John Y. Foster, *New Jersey and the Rebellion* (Newark, 1868), 865.

YMCA at that time was a relative newcomer to America and had existed in New Jersey only since 1856. Yet through the Christian Commission it rose to prominence. Through appeals to the Protestant congregations, it raised millions of dollars with which Bibles, hymnals, magazines, books, newspapers, and other supplies were purchased and distributed to the troops. Nearly five thousand volunteer "delegates" of the Commission visited in camps, hospitals, and up to the front lines, rendering any services they could. About half of these delegates were clergymen, and the other half laymen, but combined they proved immensely helpful in the war effort. This would have been impossible without the enthusiastic support of the churches. New Jersey was outstanding both in the amount of money it contributed and in the quality and number of the delegates it provided through the Commission.*

Many of the New Jersey churches were still reluctant to speak an official word against slavery. Some pastors like Dr. Albert Barnes, whose call to the First Presbyterian Church in Philadelphia started the fight which finally split his denomination, spoke out strongly for emancipation. With compelling eloquence, he cried: "The age demands it. Humanity demands it. The Bible demands it. The best interest of the nation demands it." ** Once President Lincoln signed the Emancipation Proclamation, however, late in 1862, all hesitation on the part of the churches disappeared. As far as northern citizens were concerned, that settled the matter. From then on the only question was how the "freedmen" as ex-slaves were called, were to be treated. The problem, which was no minor one, fell into the lap of the Church. When the war finally reached its bloody climax the larger denominations turned their attention to the task of reconstruction in the South.

* See Lemuel Moss, *Annals of the United States Christian Commission* (Philadelphia, 1868).
** Albert Barnes, *The Conditions of Peace* (Philadelphia, 1863), 35.

The record of that period is not a pleasant one. Opportunists both North and South were quick to take advantage of the chaos in the southern states, and the bitterness engendered during four years of war made it easy to let policy be dictated by vengeance. The assassination of Lincoln was a mortal blow to moderates in Congress and in the country as a whole. There were many of these in New Jersey, but their voice was drowned by the vindictive chorus elsewhere in the North. Nonetheless, the record of the churches was good. Even though there was the usual moral slump which always follows a war, the major denominations began efforts at once to assist the emancipated Negroes in securing sufficient education for responsible citizenship. Sometimes setting up a separate Board of Missions to the Freedmen, or making the mission to the Negro part of the Home Mission effort, the churches collected funds, enlisted teachers and sent them south to found schools. Some of the most eminent institutions of the South such as Hampton Institute in Virginia, Fisk University in Tennessee, and Howard University in Washington, D. C., had their beginnings in this fashion. Countless small Negro schools supported by northern churches began to appear in the southern states. Some of them passed out of existence as the states slowly began a free public education system, but many remain to this day as private academies and colleges devoted to the education of the Negro. The Presbyterians founded Lincoln University in Pennsylvania, the Episcopalians through the Negro Church Institute established a number of schools including St. Augustine's College in North Carolina, while the Methodists contributed several colleges such as Morris Brown College in Atlanta. To these enterprises the churches of New Jersey contributed generously.

The energy of the New Jersey churchmen was not confined to improving the lot of the Negro alone. Other domestic concerns such as missions to the American Indian, to the recent immigrants, as well as long standing social concerns like temperance and Sabbath-observance were common objects for church action in the postwar period. At the same time another concern demanded an increasing share of the resources of the various churches: the foreign missionary enterprise. By the end of the Civil War all the major Protestant denominations had missionary commitments abroad, and New Jersey supplied its full share of personnel and financial support for this purpose.

V

NEW SOCIAL CHALLENGES
1870-1914

THE CIVIL WAR was a Protestant quarrel. Such, at least, was the judgment of many Roman Catholics at the time. They took very little part in the great abolitionist debate. Further, the political power of Catholics was so limited and their presence in America for the most of them so recent that they were not greatly upset by the withdrawal of the South from the Union. They had problems enough of their own without becoming implicated in any more, and the war dissipated some of the anti-Catholic venom which had been stirred up by the Know-Nothing Party and the Native American Association. The Roman hierarchy in this country was chiefly concerned with four problems during the nineteenth century: the establishment of new churches, the securing of an adequate supply of domestic priests, the creation of a parochial school system, and Americanizing the Church.

CATHOLIC STRUGGLE AGAINST BIGOTRY

When Pius VII, in 1808, finally divided the see of Baltimore into five parts, making Baltimore an archdiocese with four suffragan dioceses under it, he divided New Jersey, as we might have suspected, between the diocese of New York and the diocese of Philadelphia. At that time there was not a single organized Roman Catholic parish in the State. Indeed, it was not until 1814 that the first church was erected, St. John's in Trenton, and the second, St. John's Church in Paterson, was not begun until 1821. In part this was due to the paucity of Catholics and in part to the militant anti-Catholic bias of many of their Protestant neighbors. When services were begun in New Brunswick, this notice appeared in *The Protestant:*

Popish delusion and fanaticism are equally degrading as that of the heathen nations, and just as pernicious. To prove this we have only to behold the wonderful perversion of Scripture exhibited on the front of the new mass house in New Brunswick. On a piece of marble is this inscription—"Thou art Peter, and upon this rock will I build my church, and the gates of hell shall not prevail against it." *

Since most of the Catholics were recent immigrants to the state, an organization known as the Native American Association was formed to keep foreigners out of public office and prevent their easy naturalization. Though they professed, "We war against no religious institution or denomination," it was clear that they had a strong anti-Catholic viewpoint. Their chief effort was to secure an alteration of the naturalization laws so that twenty-one years' residence would be required to obtain citizenship, but there is no doubt that they also helped stir up feeling against Catholic immigrants.** In addition inflammatory pamphlets were circulated with such warnings as

Americans do no longer deceive yourselves. . . . The cry is: where is the danger? What can the Papists do? Hearken! Now Popery controls the press in a direct and in an indirect way! Now Popery balances the power in the elections wherever it throws its weight in the political scale. In ten years, Jesuits

* *The Protestant*, I, No. 41, 324.
** See *Constitution and By-Laws of the Native American Association of the Township of Camden* (Camden, 1844).

will control America in religious power! And in twenty, they will plant the Inquisition. . . . This is what the Pope and the Jesuits aim at.*

This sort of propaganda often leads to violence, and in New York and Philadelphia violence was touched off. What is remarkable, however, is the relative absence of such outbreaks in New Jersey. In the 1850's a crowd of roughnecks led by members of the Know-Nothing Party tried to tear down the Catholic Church in Elizabethtown. The priest, Father Howell, heard about it before the mob arrived and realized that if his men tried to defend the place bloodshed would probably follow. Therefore, he sent all the men home and allowed their womenfolk, with children in arms, to confront the advancing throng. Fortunately, chivalry was not dead, so the crowd finally dispersed after vainly trying to get the women to leave the church.**

Gradually more parishes were organized and more churches were built until the number of Catholics warranted the creation of a new diocese. In 1853 the parishes in New Jersey were removed from the dioceses of New York and Philadelphia and incorporated into the Diocese of Newark. Altogether there were 33 churches in the state. The first bishop, James Roosevelt Bayley, was ordained originally in the Episcopal Church and later became converted to Roman Catholicism. His selection as bishop proved to be a happy choice for his diocese. In addition to establishing new parishes, he set about founding a college to provide Catholic higher education and particularly to train new priests. The result was the beginning of Seton Hall College in 1856, named for Bishop Bayley's aunt, the famed Mother Elizabeth Seton, herself a convert, who was founder of the American

* L. Giustiniani, *Intrigues of Jesuitism in the U.S.A.* (Camden, 1846), 81.
** Joseph M. Flynn, *The Catholic Church in New Jersey* (Morristown, 1904), 144.

James Roosevelt Bayley, first Bishop of Newark and eighth
Archbishop of Baltimore, in a portrait by Healey
From The Life of James Roosevelt Bayley
by Sister M. Hildegarde Yaeger, 1947

branch of the Sisters of Charity of St. Vincent de Paul.
Originally located near Madison, the College was moved
to South Orange in 1860, at which time a seminary course
for the priesthood was begun.

Another concern of Bishop Bayley was to secure several teaching orders of nuns to staff his parochial school system. When the Catholics organized their parishes, they found the public school system already in operation in most of the towns where Catholic churches were located. The idea of free education for all was looked on as a great boon by the immigrant families settling over here, most of whom had been deprived of educational opportunities in the countries from which they had come. But to the hierarchy the public schools were anathema. Staffed with Protestant teachers, using textbooks written by Protestants, and with a majority of the students Protestant, these public schools looked like veiled instruments of proselytizing. So, almost from the start, the Catholic bishops determined to set up their own school system. The cost of such an enterprise was very high, and many of the loyal Catholic laity complained. It was particularly distasteful to Catholic parents in view of the fact that they had to pay taxes for the public schools whether they sent their children there or not. Repeated attempts were made by the hierarchy to secure public funds to assist the parochial school system, but each time they were defeated.

Every so often the issue would erupt in the pages of the press, as happened in Jersey City in 1853. It was sparked by a letter to the editor of the *Daily Telegraph* from Father Kelly of St. Peter's Church urging that, since a quarter of the school children of Jersey City were in parochial schools, some tax relief should be afforded. At once he was answered by Dr. Alexander McClure, Pastor of the First Dutch Reformed Church in the city, who in effect asked why not send Catholic children to the public schools?

Nothing prevents their attendance except the facts that the peculiar religion of Rome is not taught in them, and that they are conducted on *the only plan* which is perfectly impartial towards all the different orders of Protestants, as well as towards the adherents of Rome.*

This, of course, is precisely what the Catholics denied. As long as the King James Version of the Bible was read, they contended, the public schools could not be impartial. What makes that literary exchange so interesting today is the fact that the same debate continues to break out periodically.

Though the bishops were unsuccessful in securing tax help for their parochial schools, they were able to get their people to assume the costs of building and maintaining them. Usually pressure had to be brought to bear to secure support for this project. Some parents were reluctant to pay tuition for their children, and some felt that the quality of education in the parochial schools was considerably below that of the public institutions. Bishops at times threatened excommunication of parents who refused to send their children to the church school, or as Bishop Michael J. O'Farrell of Trenton did, refused to confirm children who attended public school.**

Bishop Bayley was noted for two other events in his episcopate. In 1864 he was able to get a law passed by the State Legislature making it possible to incorporate Roman Catholic property.† Though it cannot be proved, it is likely that this was a *quid pro quo* in return for Catholic volunteers to the Union Army and the support of the Roman Church for the war effort. This act of incorporation was an important step in the suppression of trusteeism in the Catholic parishes of New Jersey: an attempt on the part of the laity to secure the right to select their priests and control church property. Although trusteeism was never the problem in New Jersey

* *The School Question: A Correspondence Between Rev. J. Kelly and Rev. A. W. McClure, Jersey City* (New York, 1853), 6, 18.

** It was this latter which prompted Reverend M. V. McDuffie, a pastor in New Brunswick, to write his *Light for Protestants and Catholics* (New Brunswick, 1890).

† See *Acts of the 88th Legislature of the State of N. J.* (Newark, 1864), 57-58.

that it became in New York, it did create unrest in some congregations like St. Peter's Church in New Brunswick. The other notable event was Bishop Bayley's participation in the First Vatican Council. Unlike the Second Council ninety-three years later, the bishops who attended had only a vague idea of its purpose or the matters they were to discuss. When it became known that the question of papal infallibility was on the agenda, Bayley was one of 20 American bishops who petitioned Pius IX not to bring the matter up for discussion. It was not a question of disbelief. In a letter home, he wrote, "With the exception of a *very* few we all believe in the Infallibility of the Pope teaching ex cathedra." * But he feared the result such a dogma would have upon public opinion at home.

CATHOLICS AND IMMIGRATION

Following the Civil War, industrial expansion in America coupled with social upheavals in Europe led to a step-up in United States immigration. In this development New Jersey received its full share of newcomers. The immigration was not an unmixed blessing, however. For one thing it began to change the national-origins balance within the state which caused alarm on the part of dominant groups. In 1850 only 12 per cent of the population of New Jersey was foreign born. By 1870 the percentage had jumped to 21, and it was 23 per cent by 1890. Furthermore, the influx swelled the urban areas. During the twenty-year period from 1850 to 1870 Essex County more than doubled in population while Hudson County increased 600 per cent. On the other hand, counties like Hunterdon, Sussex, and Monmouth grew very little, if at all.** A very high proportion of the immigrants were Roman Catholic. Almost all the Irish and a

* Quoted in M. Hildegarde Yaeger, *The Life of James Roosevelt Bayley* (Washington, 1947), 260-262.
** *Geological Survey of New Jersey, 1895* (Trenton, 1898), IV, Appendix, 152 f.

majority of the Germans were of that faith, and together they formed the bulk of the waves of immigration up to 1880.

The Protestants of New Jersey looked on this invasion with scarcely concealed distaste. Associating Catholicism with the oppressive regimes in Spain, Austria, and Italy, they immediately assumed that the Catholic immigrants bore with them the seeds of clerical autocracy. In a speech before the Order of United Americans in Jersey City, James K. Cook expressed the views of many Protestants at that time:

We must not suffer the liberality of our institutions to be shackled by the despotism and intolerant policy which governs in the dominions of the Pope of Rome, and which prevails in all Catholic countries.*

Nor were Protestants the only ones disturbed by the immigration. The Catholic hierarchy viewed the incoming flood with just as serious misgivings. It was hard enough to supply churches and schools for the resident Catholics without straining their resources further to care for the impoverished newcomers. In addition to church facilities, the immigrants needed food, clothing, jobs, houses, in fact just about everything necessary for human survival. Many of them had to learn a new language, and all had to learn the laws and customs of their adopted homeland. It was a task to make the stoutest quail. Yet the Roman Catholic leaders set about to accomplish the job, and while they were far from completely successful, the degree to which they achieved their purpose is a standing testimony to their ability and devotion.

Meanwhile, the Protestant churches, as churches, did little to assist the immigrants. Since the bulk were Roman Catholics, it was assumed the problem was a Catholic one. Not until well into the twentieth century was an attempt

* James K. Cook, *Addresses Delivered Before Charter Oak Chapter No. 19, Order of United Americans of New Jersey* (New York, 1855), 28.

made by some Protestant communions to establish missions for the immigrant. One unfortunate result of this was to separate further Protestants and Catholics. Except in business affairs the two communities remained quite distinct. As a consequence whenever the two engaged in controversy it was all too often a case of one side trying to shout down the other without really meeting the problems raised. For example, when, in 1875, the Reverend Elijah Lucas, Pastor of the First Baptist Church in Trenton, preached a sermon on Catholicism to the American Protestant Association, it was filled with violent verbiage such as, "no Roman Catholic could be a good citizen" and the Jesuits are "a class worse than the lice of Egypt." An account of the speech was published in the *Evening Journal* and elicited an angry reply from the Reverend Patrick Byrne, Dean of St. John's Roman Catholic Church in Trenton. For several weeks thereafter the two clerics carried on a running debate with each other through the press. They never once met in person, nor did their arguments actually answer one another even though each liberally sprinkled his letters with expletives. When Lucas raised the issue of papal infallibility and the Syllabus of Errors, Father Byrne called this "vile and slanderous abuse of the Catholic Church." Also, when questions of biblical versus papal authority were raised, Byrne called them "ornamental appendages of this wanton, ungenerous, and unmanly asault." *

In the same way, when the Dean asked how there could be a multiplicity of Baptist denominations with conflicting beliefs if the Baptists had the truth, Lucas' only reply was to refer to the "terrible Popish outrages" and to ask rhetorically, "Where is there a particle of difference between the *idolatry* of the *heathen,* and the idolatry of the Romanist?" ** In short, one gets the impression that

* *The Great Controversy upon Catholicism and Protestantism* (Trenton, 1875), 5, 60. St. John's Roman Catholic Church, Trenton, was renamed Sacred Heart shortly after this.
** *The Great Controversy upon Catholicism and Protestantism* (Trenton, 1875), 40.

neither party was actually speaking to the other. Rather, he was addressing his own constituents. Perhaps this was due in part to the fact that the spirit of the times was against honest and open debate. Not for another eighty-five years would it be possible to substitute real discussion for rank invective.

The influx of Catholic immigrants brought about new diocesan changes. When Bishop Michael A. Corrigan, who succeeded Bishop Bayley, was elevated to the position of Archbishop of New York, the Newark diocese was split in 1881 to form the Diocese of Trenton in the south under Bishop Michael J. O'Farrell, and the Diocese Newark covered the northern half of the State under Bishop Winand M. Wigger. The latter unintentionally became the center of a dispute which agitated American Catholics toward the end of the century. It was occasioned by the desire of many of the immigrant Catholics to have bishops and priests of their own nationality over them. They suggested that dioceses be set up not according to geographical units but rather according to nationality groups. The proponents of this plan argued that tens of thousands of Catholics had been lost to the Church, because they did not feel at home with priests from another nationality. The movement soon identified itself with the St. Raphael Society, an organization set up by a German merchant named Peter Cahensly, to protect Catholic emigrants. Bishop Wigger, who was himself of German ancestry, became president of the St. Raphael Society in New York and expressed some interest in Cahensly's suggestion to create nationality groups. When the German priests organized a *Priester-Verein* and met in Newark, they did so with Wigger's blesing. The other bishops of the American hierarchy meanwhile came out in strong opposition to Cahensly's scheme, and eventually the Pope denounced it, but not before Bishop Wigger extricated himself from implication in the movement.* The whole episode revealed some of the strong feelings

* See Joseph M. Flynn, *The Catholic Church in New Jersey* (Morristown, 1904), 490-494.

of dislike which separated the German from the Irish Catholics and the struggle for power between the two. Of course the other American bishops were right in their determination to kill Cahensly's plan. If Catholicism were to grow in America, it must cease being a foreign import and become thoroughly Americanized. The continued growth of the Roman communion in the United States is ample proof that their aim was a wise one.

RISE OF AMERICAN JUDAISM

Another religious community that was greatly influenced by the tides of immigration in the nineteenth century was the Jewish one. The record of Jews in New Jersey prior to the 1840's is very scanty. There were no synagogues at all; the practicing Jews had to relate themselves to one of the New York congregations. Indeed, not until the revolutions in Europe drove out many German Jews was there any substantial settlement of Jews in New Jersey. Then suddenly synagogues were organized and congregations formed. The first was the Congregation B'nai Jeshurun in Paterson which dates from 1847, and the Newark congregation which appeared a year later. Both congregations maintained close ties with New York Jews, and requested aid from them on several occasions. The Paterson congregation asked for the loan of a *sefer torah* in 1849, and in Newark a request was made for financial help in purchasing a cemetery and building the first synagogue.* Sometime in the 1850's a congregation was organized in New Brunswick, and it was not until 1860 that we hear of a synagogue in Trenton, even though Jews had been living there since the 1840's.** Just as the Newark Jews relied on New York, so those in Trenton looked for aid from Philadelphia where a fairly large Jewish population centered.

* See Hyman B. Grinstein, *The Rise of the Jewish Community of New York* (Philadelphia, 1945), 523.
** Harry J. Podmore, "Trenton," *Universal Jewish Encyclopedia*, X, 300-303.

When the Civil War broke out, the Jews, as a body, took no position either for or against slavery, leaving the decision to the individual.* There were a number who were highly critical of the northern attitude toward slavery. One of these was David Naar, one of the most prominent Jews of his day. For a time he served as mayor of Elizabeth and also was a judge in Essex County. While he was an ardent Democrat, he left politics and entered the newspaper business in 1853 when he purchased *The True American,* a daily paper in Trenton. His criticisms of Lincoln's Administration and of the war effort as a whole raised such a storm that for a time he was forced to suspend publication.** On the other hand there were a number of Jews who had a strong concern for abolition. Some of these were recent immigrants from Germany where they had absorbed some of the radical social theories of the left-wing movements in Europe.

In 1880 began another great wave of immigration, with many Russian and Polish Jews among the newcomers. By this time the older group of immigrants was well settled and many of them were fairly prosperous. They viewed with a certain degree of consternation the idea of providing a place in their midst for this army of impoverished refugees. The dimensions of this invasion may be grasped in the census figures. During the two decades between 1880 and 1900 the number of Jews in New Jersey alone increased 500 per cent.† It was a relief, then, when the idea of establishing agricultural communities in unoccupied areas of the United States was suggested. The plan made sense, because most of the immigrants had been farm laborers in Russia and Poland and so would

* Max J. Kohler, "The Jews and the American Anti-Slavery Movement," *Publications of the American Jewish Historical Society,* No. 5 (1897), 143.

** Harry J. Podmore, "Trenton," *Universal Jewish Encyclopedia,* X, 300-303.

† From 5600 to over twenty-five thousand. See Joshua O. Haberman, *The Jews in New Jersey* (MS in Rutgers University Library); and Abram S. Isaacs, "New Jersey," *The Jewish Encyclopedia,* IX, 241f.

feel more at home in a country environment than in the city. Besides it solved the problem of having illiterate and poverty-stricken neighbors in the already overcrowded Jewish sections of the Eastern cities. Many New Jersey congregations contributed generously to the Hebrew Immigrant Aid Society of New York which supported the colonization idea. Before long colonies had been planted in such widely separated areas as Louisiana, South Dakota, Colorado, Oregon, Kansas, Michigan, Virginia, Connecticut, and New Jersey. Within a few years, however, all the colonies ceased to function except those in New Jersey, and the reason the latter lasted longer than the others was the proximity of Jewish congregations in Philadelphia which continued to support them until they were well established. Elsewhere, the colonies were located far from any Hebrew center, or source of encouragement and support. On the other hand, of the nine New Jersey colonies, four survived into the 1940's.*

JEWISH AGRICULTURAL COLONIES

The first colony founded in 1882 was located about four miles northwest of Vineland. It was named Alliance after the *Alliance Israélite Universelle,* an international Jewish organization centered in Paris which aided refugee Jews and provided help for the colony. Scrub woodland was bought, and it was here that farms were laid out for the settlers. Living was communal style for several years until individual houses could be built. When crop failure almost caused the extinction of the colony, financial assistance was provided by the Association of Jewish Immigrants, a benevolent society set up by Hebrew congregations in Philadelphia.** In the same year that Alliance was begun two other Jewish communities were started nearby. Rosenhayn was also sponsored by the Hebrew

* Peter Wiernik, *History of the Jews in America* (New York, 1931), 268 f.
** Philip R. Goldstein, *Social Aspects of the Jewish Colonies of South Jersey* (New York, 1921), 13-15.

Immigrant Society, and Carmel was founded by a Polish Jew named Michael Heilprin. Six years later still another agricultural colony was located at Garton Road in Cumberland County. All of these had hard going for a time, and when small industries were started in the neighborhood, most of the colonists deserted the farm to work in

Interior of Eben Ha'Ezer Synagogue at Alliance, 1889
Reprinted from Kelin's "Migdal Zophim" in Yoval, 1932

the industrial plants. By far the most ambitious of these colonies was the one established through the support of the Baron de Hirsch Fund at Woodbine, New Jersey. Baron Maurice de Hirsch, a German philanthropist who used most of his fortune to assist immigrant Jews from Eastern Europe, established a special fund in New York with capital resources of $2,400,000, later enlarged to $4,000,000. The income from this fund was used to assist the Jewish immigrants who were arriving by the boat-load at this time. In 1891 the Fund purchased three thousand acres of land in south Jersey and began a Jew-ish farm settlement there. Later the tract was enlarged to 5800 acres, and in 1895 the Woodbine Agricultural School was founded. Yearly grants from the Fund enabled the colony to flourish, though the farm settlement was never very successful. As industry grew up around the colony, more people worked in industry than farmed.

In 1903 the colony was incorporated as a borough, the first all-Jewish community in the United States. Gradu-ally other settlers moved in, until by 1940 only 40 per cent of the Woodbine residents were Jewish. Synagogues were established in all the Jewish colonies of south Jersey, but none had a resident rabbi. A ritual slaughterer was the only professional in any of the synagogues. Beyond this, the colonies had to call on the resources of the con-gregations in Philadelphia. By the late 1940's all the colonies had ceased to operate as communal settlements. The land by this time was all privately owned and the other community asets of the colonies were turned over to the boroughs near by. The Woodbine Agricultural School was surrendered to the State in 1917 to found a home for the feeble-minded.* In the end, one of the chief purposes of the colonization plan failed. Only a few hundred immigrants were willing to begin life again on the farm, and thus most of the farm colonies were forced to disband. The majority of the immigrants settled down in the city, near their port of entry and created Jewish communities within those cities. Here they lived quite apart from their Gentile neighbors in areas which in-creasingly took on the characteristics of the European ghettos from which many of the Jews had come. This was most often true of the Orthodox Jews who tended to estab-

* See Sherry Abel, "Woodbine," *Universal Jewish Encyclopedia*, X, 501 f.

lish such a close bond between their religion and the culture of the European ghetto that they could not see the difference between the two. Not all the immigrants were of that viewpoint, however. In Germany a movement had already gained strength to divorce talmudic legislation from Jewish life. The Reform movement, as it came to be called, spread to América with the German immigration and gave rise to Reform Judaism. Led by such rabbis as Isaac Mayer Wise and David Einhorn, both the worship and way of life of many American Jews was radically altered. Rabbi Wise was passionately concerned to Americanize his people, with the result that many of the old distinctive characteristics were abandoned and the form of Judaism which emerged was little different from middle-class liberal Protestantism.*

The movement toward Reform went so far in removing all distinctions from Judaism that a reaction was bound to occur, and it did when Conservative Judaism appeared as a sort of compromise between the Orthodox and Reform positions. The Conservative movement began in New York. It embodied a desire to keep as many distinctions as possible and at the same time undergird them with theological principles. It was hoped that in this way the Jewish faith would retain its distinctive character and yet enable the Jews to become good American citizens. This approach proved especially attractive to well-established, middle-class Jews, particularly in New Jersey. Whereas in 1890 four-fifths of the synagogues in the State were Orthodox with the remaining fifth Reform,** by 1960 there were more Conservative Temples than Orthodox and Reform combined.† This figure stands in interesting contrast to the national distribution which shows the Orthodox group somewhat larger than the Conservative.‡

* Nathan Glazer, *American Judaism* (Chicago, 1957), 46.
** Engelman, "Jewish Statistics in the U.S. Census of Religious Bodies (1850-1936)," *Jewish Social Studies*, IX, No. 2, 137-138.
† *The Standard American-Jewish Directory*, 1960, 106-123.
‡ Edwin S. Gaustad, *Historical Atlas of Religion in America* (New York, 1962), 146.

The period following the Civil War was a time of testing for the major Protestant denominations. The wounds they had sustained needed time to heal, and internal stresses kept their attention largely on domestic matters. Since most of the immigrants who came to New Jersey were either Roman Catholic or Jewish, the Protestants with an almost audible sigh of relief allowed the resident Catholic and Jewish communities to shoulder all responsibility for solving the problems of the immigrant. Consequently, the Roman and Jewish congregations grew at a surprising rate while the Protestant denominations remained relatively static. Not until the second decade of the twentieth century was any extensive work done by Protestant groups on behalf of immigrants. The problems which occupied the Protestant during this time can be grouped in three areas: the disunity of the Church, the rapid urbanization of the State, and the challenge of new intellectual currents from abroad. In addition the foreign missions enterprise and the temperance campaign fully occupied most of the energy and resources of the churches.

Presbyterians Seek Reunion

The Presbyterians were painfully conscious, especially in New Jersey, that they were a divided church long before the war, and those divisions had been accentuated by the conflict. While the Old School–New School schism had been healed in the South by 1864, it was still very much alive in the North, even though many were eager to bring the two northern branches together again. In 1862 the Old School Assembly adopted a resolution suggesting that the two General Assemblies exchange commissioners, and the following year the New School Assembly agreed and forthwith appointed delegates. The exchange strengthened the desire for complete union so that when the Old School Assembly met in Newark, in 1864, a spontaneous meeting was held to promote that end. Two years later both Assemblies met in St. Louis and began active steps toward reunion.* It was not all sweetness and light, however. Charles Hodge of Princeton Seminary vigorously attacked the proposed union in an article in the *Princeton Review* on the basis that the New School did not accept the Westminster Confession of Faith in a Reformed or Calvinistic sense.** By this he apparently meant the sense exhibited in his massive three-volume systematic theology. The rest of the Church was not convinced by this, especially when such New School leaders as Professor H. B. Smith of Union Seminary heartily subscribed to the confessional statement "in the Calvinistic or Reformed sense." By vote of the Presbyteries the union was approved and took place in the spring of 1869 to the vast relief of the majority of the Church. The greater schism, that between the North and the South, was not so easily healed. A few tentative motions were made by the northern Church, but the South was too bitter and too chaotic to respond favorably. So the Church remained divided, and continues so to the present time. In New Jersey, however, the Presbyterians were now one united body again after 1869 and were ready to face the problems of urbanization and intellectual ferment.

Like most of the Protestant comunions, the Presbyterians at first seemed unaware of the social revolution going on around them. With the rapid spread of the factory system and the great influx of immigrants, the old social framework was put to severe test. Before the advent of the factory most Americans were able to live within the framework of Jeffersonian individualism. This was the framework within which the churches also operated, so that their concern was chiefly with individual salvation. But individualism did not work in a factory, as the day laborer soon found out. He was dependent on the whim of the boss for the job which meant his daily bread. Few Presbyterians, however, were conscious of this, because

* William Adams, "The Reunion," Chapter V in *Presbyterian Re-Union Memorial Volume* (New York, 1870).
** *The Biblical Repertory and Princeton Review,* XL (1868), 420 ff.

the Presbyterian denomination—like most of the major Protestant churches—was a church of farmers and of the upper and middle classes in industry. The factory workers were usually Roman Catholics or Jews. Not until after 1910 was any serious consideration given to the problems of the working-class Christian.

But while the Presbyterians were slow to respond to the industrial challenge, they were among the first to react to the new intellectual currents of the age. In Europe the rapid growth of scientific knowledge led to theories which appeared to strike at the heart of the Christian message. Evolution seemed to destroy the uniqueness of man so that instead of being "little lower than the angels" he was seen as little higher than the apes. Materialism asserted that reality is found only in the material world which is subject to sense perception, thus ruling out God and the whole spiritual realm. And determinism replaced Divine Providence with a purpose-less chain of cause and effect. As if this were not enough, German universities began a critical study of the Scriptures and challenged the whole concept of divine inspiration.

As these ideas slowly filtered into the colleges and seminaries, they produced a veritable storm in which New Jersey again became a battleground. Princeton Theological Seminary stood out as the seat of orthodoxy and refused to admit any of the new ideas. This was understandable, because the whole magnificent edifice of the Princeton theology rested on the premise that the Bible is free of all error. Dr. Charles Hodge stated the case in its baldest terms at the fiftieth anniversary of his professorship in 1877: "I am not afraid to say," he commented, "that a new idea never originated in this Seminary." * The reason for this astonishing claim was the simple belief Hodge had that his theology was merely an orderly statement of what the Bible has already said. Therefore

* Robert H. Nichols, "Charles Hodge," *Dictionary of American Biography*, IX, 98. See Lefferts A. Loetscher, *The Broadening Church* (Philadelphia, 1957), 25.

innovation would be anathema. Hodge, however, refused to apply to the Bible the same critical judgment which he applied to everything else. He took the Bible as it was and refused to speculate upon its derivations. Union Seminary in New York had no such scruples. Led by Dr. Charles Augustus Briggs, an eminent scholar in his own right, that seminary took an increasingly sympathetic view of biblical criticism and attacked the "scholastic theology" that was taught at Princeton. For a number of years the views of these two schools were aired in a joint publication, *The Presbyterian Review*, but as their positions moved farther and farther apart, the journal was finally abandoned in 1889.* In 1892 Briggs was charged with heresy and a year later was suspended from the ministry of the Presbyterian Church by action of the General Assembly. Refusing to dismiss him from his professorial chair, Union Seminary withdrew from Presbyterian control and became a nondenominational institution. The controversy had its effect on the Presbyterian churches of New Jersey, as Union graduates filled the pulpits in the northern part of the State, while Princeton graduates commanded the southern and central sectors. Gradually, the controversy between the two parties hardened until it erupted into the modernist-fundamentalist battle following World War I.

EPISCOPALIANS FACE SCHISM

In 1899 Dr. Briggs applied to Bishop Henry Potter, of the New York Diocese of the Episcopal Church, for ordination, and to the amazement of many was accepted and ordained. This threw the controversy into the Episcopal camp. It was not the first time the question of biblical higher criticism had been faced in that communion, for the Mother Church in England had been embroiled with the question for a number of decades. There were protests all over the Church against the ad-

* For a detailed discussion of the controversy, see Lefferts A. Loetscher, *The Broadening Church* (Philadelphia, 1957), Chapter 4.

mission of Briggs, but the issue never produced quite the storm it did among the Presbyterians. One reason is that the Episcopalians had just emerged from a struggle between their High Church and Low Church parties. Thanks to the influence of Bishop Doane and men like him, New Jersey Episcopalians were largely High Church. This was not true of most of the Episcopal churches of the inland states. Many of them were emphatically Low Church and determined to keep the Anglo-Catholics from places of authority. As late as 1874 the General Convention passed an amendment to its canon law forbidding the elevation of the elements in Holy Communion, genuflection, bowing, and "all other acts not authorized by the Rubrics of the Book of Common Prayer." * The High Churchmen just ignored the provisions and continued to make the Church more Catholic. A number of Low Churchmen who protested this development were deposed, such as the Reverend Marshall B. Smith of New Jersey who was deposed by his High Church Bishop William Odenheimer for communing with the Dutch Reformed Church. Finally, a revolt directed by Bishop George D. Cummins of Kentucky led a number of the Low Churchmen to break with the Protestant Episcopal connection and to establish the Reformed Episcopal Church in 1873. Since part of the dispute revolved around the wording of services in the Book of Common Prayer, the leaders of the revolt adopted the "Proposed Book of Common Prayer" which the Episcopalians had rejected in 1785. Before they adopted it, however, Cummins made several drastic changes in its wording to remove anything that smacked of sacerdotalism or of a High view of the sacraments. To the disappointment of Cummins and his few associates, most of the Low Churchmen preferred to stay in the main church and strongly deplored the move toward schism.** As a result,

* James T. Addison, *The Episcopal Church in the United States* (New York, 1951), 210.
** E. Clowes Chorley, *Men and Movements in the American Episcopal Church* (Hamden, Conn., 1961), Chapter XIV.

the Reformed Episcopalians remained small in numbers, never reaching more than 90 congregations and finally declining to the present 64.

Despite the schism, the Episcopal Church in New Jersey continued to grow in number of parishes and communicants until the diocese had to be divided into two. The northern part of the State was incorporated into the Diocese of Newark and the southern into the continuing Diocese of New Jersey. The Catholic element in the church, meanwhile, flourished even more. Religious orders for Episcopal monks and nuns were founded with houses being opened in Newark, Jersey City, and Mendham.** In worship, the invocation of the saints, the service of the Benediction of the Blessed Sacrament, and the use of eucharistic vestments became increasingly common. Those clergy who did not sympathize with this development either kept their peace or left to join another denomination. A number entered the Methodist Church in this way, finding there the Low Church Episcopal service in which they felt most at home.

TENSIONS IN OTHER CHURCHES

The Methodists, meanwhile, had been showing a steady growth in New Jersey. They were changing in other ways as well. Following the Civil War many of the New Jersey congregations were large enough to support a full-time minister so that the circuit system was no longer suitable for them. Furthermore, as church members rose economically, from the laboring class to the middle-management bracket, they became more sophisticated and demanded a better-trained ministry. Good as the "saddle-bag school" had been in training preachers for the frontier, it was scarcely adequate to providing an educated ministry for city churches. As a result the New Jersey Conference opened a theological seminary at Madison in 1867. The leaders of the church were able to secure the support of Daniel Drew, a New York financier, to

* *The Episcopal Church Annual, 1963* (New York, 1962), 128-131.

launch the venture with an initial grant of $250,000 and promise of millions more in endowment. In appreciation the school was named Drew Seminary. That in itself was a commentary on the times, since Daniel Drew was notorious for some of the most shameless financial schemes of the era. · In company with Jay Gould and James Fisk, he was involved in one shady stock deal after another, and at the same time he was a devout Methodist. Ironically, his fortune disappeared as quickly as it had grown, and Drew died a pauper; hence the Seminary to which he had given his name never received the promised endowment.*

Another issue which occupied Methodist attention during this period was that of lay representation at the General Conference. This was one of the questions, it will be recalled, that helped bring on the Methodist Protestant schism in 1828. As Nicholas Snethen had prophesied, the agitation for more representative government in the Methodist Episcopal Church would never die until it was satisfied. His prophecy proved correct, but it was not until 1872 that sufficient ministerial votes were secured to change the rules of Conference in order to allow two lay delegates from each Annual Conference to be members of General Conference. It was, as one historian put it, "the completion of the Americanization of Methodism." ** As long as the Church continued split, however, it was not completely American. A number of the ministers who had split off in 1843 to form the Wesleyan Connection returned to the Methodist Church after the war, since the original reason for their departure —slavery—was now removed. The problem of reuniting the northern and southern branches was far more difficult. It began in earnest when, in 1876, five commissioners from each church met for a week at Cape May to discuss the matter. No reunion plans were considered at the time,

* Allan Nevins, "Daniel Drew," *Dictionary of American Biography*, V, 450-451.
** Halford E. Luccock and Paul Hutchinson, *The Story of Methodism* (New York, 1926), 372.

there was only the cordial exchange of fraternal greetings. Neither church was ready for merger just yet. That would have to wait for another sixty-three years.

While the Methodists continued to grow in numbers, several Protestant churches merely held their own or lost ground in New Jersey. The Baptist churches, which had had a spectacular period of growth up to the 1920's, suddenly leveled off and thereafter scarcely kept pace with the growth of population. This can be explained partly by the emigration of many Baptists westward to the frontier, but even more by the fact that the loose polity and informality of the Baptist church was far more suited to farm communities than to urban ones. As industrialism spread across the State, the Baptist growth was arrested.* The Dutch Reformed were bound by their continued ties, culturally at least, with the Netherlands, so that few of non-Dutch descent cared to join that communion. The Lutheran Church had never been very strong in New Jersey, centering for the most part on Philadelphia. The German immigrants who came over just after the Civil War were predominantly Roman Catholics and so did not provide many additions to the Lutheran or German Reformed communions. The Society of Friends declined in numbers, but its members remained very active in community life. They were especially noted for their academies and colleges, though none was located in New Jersey. The Congregational Church, which was notably absent from New Jersey from 1801 until after the Civil War began to establish a few congregations in the northern part of the state during the latter part of the century. Largely, this was to accommodate New Englanders who, for commercial or other reasons, moved to New Jersey. But Congregationalism never became very strong. Another New England export was the Unitarian Society. The first Unitarian

* Cf. Henry C. Vedder, *A History of the Baptists in the Middle States* (Philadelphia, 1898), Chapter XI; Norman Maring, *A History of New Jersey Baptists* (Unpublished MS held by New Jersey Baptist Convention, East Orange), Chapter VII.

fellowship of which we have record was organized at Vineland in 1865. Not much is known of this group though it continued active until 1935, when it was disbanded.* Not until 1889 was another Unitarian church founded, when the First Unitarian Society of Plainfield came into being. The Seventh Day Baptist Church offered its facilities to the new organization, but this arrangement did not last very long. Not only was the liberal teaching of the Unitarians scandalous to the orthodox trinitarians of Plainfield, but the Unitarian preacher, the Reverend Robert Collyer, made an unhappy reference to the various denominations as resembling different rooms in a great house. The Unitarians were the sun room, the Presbyterians the blue room, and the Baptists the bathroom! Thereafter the Unitarians had to find different quarters.** Before 1900 Unitarian societies had been formed in Orange, Rutherford, Passaic, and Ridgewood. Yet growth has never been very marked, and today there are only thirteen active churches and five Unitarian fellowships in the State, most of which are located in the northeastern section.†

THE SOCIAL GOSPEL

One activity which all the Protestant churches shared in common during this period was a passion for missions. Each denomination had its mission boards to select missionary candidates and disburse the mission offerings which the individual congregations contributed. These missions were located all over the world and also among the American Indians, the Negroes of the South, the immigrants in the city, and wherever needy people were

* *Inventory of the Church Archives in New Jersey: Unitarian Church* (Newark, 1940).
** Charles A. Selden, *Semi-Centennial of the First Unitarian Society, Plainfield, N. J.* and *Notes on the Semi-Centennial of the First Unitarian Society, Plainfield, N. J., October 27th-30th, 1939* (n.p., 1939), 23.
† *Directory Unitarian-Universalist Association* (Boston, 1963), 133-135.

found. New Jersey congregations of all denominations gave full support to this enterprise, and supplied outstanding leaders such as Bishop William H. Hare of the Episcopal Church, who was born in Princeton and worked most of his life among the Indians in the Dakotas, or Samuel Zwemer, who went from New Brunswick Seminary to start a new mission in Arabia. No other activity of the Church consumed as much of the energy and resources of Protestant Christians as did the missionary movement. While the world was not evangelized in one generation, it certainly was profoundly changed. The sudden emergence of new nations and peoples which has characterized the period since World War II owes much to these missionary concerns.

Another common concern of the Protestant churches was social welfare. The temperance crusade, the Salvation Army, the social gospel, all were activities in which New Jersey churches had a part. It was in the large cities first that the need for social welfare was most sharply felt. It was here that the problems of unemployment, of the foreign-born, of the conflict between capital and labor came to a focus. In the attempt of the churches to speak to these needs, it was natural that the inner-city congregations of New York and Philadelphia should take the lead. In New York St. George's Episcopal Church and the Methodist Metropolitan Temple pioneered in making available to city-dwellers a weekday program of social, educational, and recreational activities for all age groups in the 1890's. Russell Conwell's Baptist Temple in Philadelphia did much the same thing. The example of these large churches was followed with interest by a number of New Jersey congregations which felt a responsibility for the unchurched in their midst, especially those from the laboring class. As a result of this concern, the Camden Methodist Missionary Society helped found Goodwill Industries to provide work for the physically handicapped in order that they might be enabled to support themselves in dignity rather than subsist on public charity. Today this enterprise grosses many thousands of dollars annually.

One area of social need of special concern to New Jersey was migrant farm labor. As the name "Garden State" implies, New Jersey has always been noted for its farm produce. The value of its crops was greatly enhanced when canning methods made it possible to ship vegetables long distances and preserve them almost indefinitely. Late in the nineteenth century Negro laborers began to come north to help with the harvesting of vegetables. Then Spanish-speaking workers from Puerto Rico joined the seasonal work force. The pitiful condition of many of these people came to the attention of some churchwomen from Methodist and Presbyterian churches. They, in turn, set up centers for the workers, first in Burlington and Cumberland counties, and then elsewhere. This was the beginning of the migrant ministry which is now conducted by the State Council of Churches.

To be sure, there were still many congregations which held the view that the only legitimate tasks of the Church were to preach the Gospel, convert sinners, and provide worship for the faithful. But the fact that most of the working class showed little interest in Protestantism in any of its forms led some churchmen to challenge such a narrow definition of the Church's role. Unless Protestant communions could demonstrate more social concern, they would be exclusively identified with a rather narrow segment of American life.

As it turned out, the social concern prompted more questions than answers, but at least churchmen were aware that if the church were to be relevant at all it must have something to say about the great social problems of our day. Meanwhile, Protestants suddenly became aware of another sobering fact. Whereas less than 25 per cent of all church members in New Jersey had been Roman Catholics just after the Civil War, by 1914 Catholics accounted for more than half of the communicant membership of the State. Many were the dire predictions that these figures aroused. Would this mean greater tensions, less liberty, more clericalism? Could America still remain a democracy with a Catholic majority?

VI

FROM DIVERSITY TO UNITY
1914-1963

Few countries in the world can equal the United States in the number and diversity of religious sects that flourish within its bounds. In addition to the denominations imported from Europe and Britain, a bewildering variety of religious groups sprang up on American soil and spread throughout the land. Most of these, in time, took root in New Jersey, though none of national importance originated there. By far the greater number trace their origins in the State to the last decade of the nineteenth century or the first two decades of the twentieth, so that they are still relative newcomers.

RISE OF AMERICAN SECTS

Among the earliest of these groups was the Church of Christ Scientist, a religion founded by Mrs. Mary Baker Eddy in 1879. Though there were no formal congregations organized in New Jersey prior to 1900, services were being held in East Orange, Englewood, and Newark by 1897. Among the earliest practitioners was Miss Nemi Robertson, who had the distinction of being in the last class taught by Mrs. Eddy herself in 1898. Miss Robertson helped organize the congregation in Orange and practiced spiritual healing there. In 1900 six congregations were formed, and thereafter growth of the group was fairly rapid until 1950. As soon as a number of adherents sufficient to hold services is found in a locality, they may form themselves into a society and gain recognition as a branch of the Mother Church in Boston. Then when the society is able to open and maintain a reading room and fulfill certain other obligations, they may be constituted as a branch church. Since 1950 the number of churches and societies has remained fairly constant, with 64 churches and 9 societies located at present in the State. One of the most notable features of Christian Science is its practice of spiritual healing. Today there are 140 practitioners in New Jersey listed in the *Christian Science Journal* who give their full time to healing, as well as many more who serve part-time in this capacity.*

Quite a different kind of religious group that came to New Jersey about the same time is the Seventh Day Adventist Church. This body grew out of the excitement brought about by William Miller, who predicted the end of the world and the Second Coming of Christ in 1844. When the Advent failed to materialize, the prediction was reinterpreted by some of Miller's followers as referring to Christ's entering the tabernacle in heaven rather than his visible return to earth. After Miller's death in 1849 the sect was reorganized, around 1855, by O. R. L. Crozier and Mrs. Ellen Harmon White. It was not until the 1890's, however, that Seventh Day Adventist churches were founded in New Jersey; the earliest ones were at Burlington and Newark. In 1890 a camp meeting was held in Newark, and as additional congregations were established the State was organized as the New Jersey Conference in 1901. At the present time there are 40 churches and over three thousand members in the Conference.** The Adventists are noted for their observance of Saturday, or the Seventh Day, as their day of rest and worship. They also are very conservative theologically

* *Christian Science Journal* (Boston, monthly) for 1897, 1900, 1910, 1950, and 1963.
** *1963 Yearbook of Seventh Day Adventist Denomination* (Washington, 1963), 37.

and maintain a strict discipline among their members to avoid all worldliness. The liberality of their giving is proverbial. For many years they have led nearly all denominations in their per capita giving. In order to maintain their discipline and to raise their young in the tenets of their faith, the Adventists began very early to establish parochial schools. The first such school in New Jersey was begun in 1908 near Cohansey and lasted for fifty years. Today, there are seven schools maintained by the Seventh Day Adventists in New Jersey covering the first eight grades with four more covering grades one through ten. About four hundred and thirty children are enrolled in these schools. In addition they maintain an academy through the high school level at Tranquility, where about eighty students are taught.*

In 1898 a Mr. and Mrs. J. F. Brittingham of Cliffside Park began a study group to examine Baha'ism, an exotic amalgam of Shi'ite Islamic teaching, Persian gnosticism, and western liberalism. The result was the formation of the first Baha'ist Assembly in the State. In 1912 Abdul Baha', the titular leader of the sect, visited Jersey City and spoke in the Masonic Temple there. Though the group was inactive for about ten years, it was reorganized in 1937 and today Baha'i Assemblies are found in a number of New Jersey cities including Newark, Montclair, Teaneck, and New Brunswick.**

A better known and more widely spread group, the Jehovah's Witnesses, began their teaching and proselyting work in New Jersey in the late 1870's with a few Witnesses meeting in Newark. It was not until 1906, however, when they held a general convention in the Asbury Park Casino that they received much public attention. Just as it did elsewhere, their aggressive propaganda produced violent reaction. When Witnesses went from house to

* Derrel K. Smith, "Record of the Seventh Day Adventist Church Schools in New Jersey" (Unpublished thesis, Princeton Theological Seminary, 1962), 4-5.
** *Inventory of the Church Archives of New Jersey: Baha'i Assemblies* (Newark, 1940), 17-19.

house selling their literature and trying to make converts of orthodox church members, it led to the passage of laws against canvassing, handbill distribution, and disorderly conduct aimed at curbing Witness activities. The opposition was particularly acute in Hudson County during the 1930's where the Administration of "Boss" Hague jailed over one hundred Witnesses in the course of a year, on the grounds of selling books without a license and disorderly conduct. In self-defense the Witnesses turned to the higher courts to appeal the verdict of lower judicatories. In many of these instances the final verdict was in the Witnesses' favor, as in the case of *Schneider* vs. *New Jersey* in 1939. In this case an ordinance providing that every distributor of printed material must first secure a permit from the chief of police in a municipality was declared to be an abridgment of the freedom of the press and therefore unconstitutional. These battles did not endear the Witnesses to the majority of churchmen, but the sect has continued to grow until today there are 103 congregations worshiping in Kingdom Halls throughout the State with nearly ten thousand members.* The outbreaks of violence against them, which were quite common thirty years ago, have become increasingly rare.

Still another purely American religious group which penetrated New Jersey was the Church of Jesus Christ of Latter-Day Saints, popularly known as the Mormons. In 1837, shortly after the sect was founded by Joseph Smith, one of his disciples, Elder Benjamin Winchester, moved to New Egypt and made a number of converts. A Mormon Branch was organized at Hornerstown which was visited by Smith in 1840.** The Branch does not seem to have survived very long, however, and it was not until the 1920's that the Mormon faith was reintroduced in

* Information secured from Watchtower Bible and Tract Society of New York.
** Norman Maring, *A History of the New Jersey Baptists* (Unpublished MS held by New Jersey Baptist Convention, East Orange), Chapter VI, 14.

New Jersey. For a long time New Jersey was a part of the Eastern States Mission, and then it became part of the New York Stake, which is a regional division of the church. Local congregations are organized as Branches first, until they become self-supporting and can carry on all the activities of the church, at which time they become Wards. The earliest Ward in New Jersey was in Orange in the 1930's, but it was not until World War II that the group began to grow with any speed. Since then five Wards and five Branches have been formed, and in 1960 New Jersey was separated from New York and became an independent Stake. A year later the Philadelphia Stake was formed with the Camden Wards belonging to it. Growth is still not very fast, but each year the church in Salt Lake City sends missionaries to New Jersey to proselyte for the local Wards.

PENTECOSTAL WITNESS

In addition to these more unusual forms of religious expression, New Jersey provided a haven for a number of fundamentalist pentecostal type of Christian sects. Many of them began as splinter groups that broke away from Methodist or Baptist churches in the west. The chief issue in these schisms seems to have been the question of holiness or sanctification as a necessary part of Christian experience in which the Holy Spirit cleansed the believer and made it possible for him to live a perfectly holy life. This experience was usually evidenced by the ability to "speak in tongues" or to heal the sick by the laying on of hands. In addition to a highly emotional form of worship, these sects showed great zeal for witnessing, for missionary work, and for carrying the Gospel to the underprivileged. One of the earliest of these groups to begin work in New Jersey was the Christian Alliance, which in 1894 was holding meetings in Asbury Park, Trenton, and West Grove. Two years later the Christian Alliance joined with a similar organization, the International Missionary Alliance, to form the Christian and Missionary Alliance. By 1910 the number of Alliance churches had grown to ten, and today there are twenty-four. Another holiness body which spread to New Jersey was the Church of the Nazarene. Beginning with a church split in California in 1895, it became a national denomination in 1908. The earliest Nazarene churches were located at Trenton and Dover with 28 congregations now found in the State. It was not until 1938 that the first Church of God congregation was organized in New Jersey. Three years prior to that Mrs. Amy Hanley, who was pastor of a Church of God in Philadelphia, began a mission in Millville. In 1938 it was organized as a congregation under her leadership, and she continued in charge of the church until 1963, when she resigned to assume the pastorate of the church in Bridgeton. At the present time there are twelve New Jersey congregations of the Church of God divided into three districts with a combined membership of over five hundred. In addition there is a Negro district with eight Negro congregations.

One small sect with its center in New Jersey is the Pillar of Fire Church begun near the turn of the century by Mrs. Alma White, the wife of an itinerant Methodist preacher. Along with her husband she conducted revival meetings all the way from California to England. Her preaching on sanctification and her open criticisms of the Methodist Church ultimately led to estrangement from her husband and departure from her Methodist connection. In 1901 she organized the Pentecostal Union Church in Denver, Colorado, later known as the Pillar of Fire. In 1906 she got a farm near Bound Brook which she named Zarephath. Unlike the founders of most pentecostal groups, Mrs. White was a prolific writer, penning many books, magazines, pamphlets, and brochures. This publicity was in large measure responsible for the securing of funds by which a college, named the Alma White College, a preparatory school, and a bible seminary were begun. In 1931 the Pillar of Fire began regular broadcasts over their new station WAWZ, consisting mostly of evangelistic services and classical music. Though the constituency of the movement has not grown appreciably in New Jersey, the one thousand-acre estate where Zarephath is located has become a self-sustaining community with farming, dairying, a printing press, and other activities caring for the needs of the resident members. Mrs. White, or Bishop White as she came to be known, died in 1946, but leadership of the organization she founded was taken over by her son, Arthur K. White.*

ORTHODOXY: THE FOURTH FAITH

In addition to the many newly-founded American sects which added to the religious diversity of New Jersey, mention should be made of the beginnings in the State of a very old form of Christianity, the Eastern Orthodox family of churches. Among the immigrants who came to America during the 1880's were a number of Greeks, Syrians, and Russians belonging to the Orthodox Church. Unfortunately, very few priests came with them so that many had to do without the services of their own communion. This was certainly true of those who settled in New Jersey. The only way for them to take part in an Orthodox service before 1900 was to go to New York City. The first Greek Orthodox Church in New Jersey was organized in Newark by the Reverend Leonidas Adamakos in 1904. Not until World War I broke out in Europe, driving more Greeks to this country, did the second church open its doors in Highland Park in 1916; another one was organized in Perth Amboy the following year. The greatest growth of the Greek Church came between 1922 and 1940 after the Russian Revolution and the massacres of the Greeks by the Turks. At the present time there are fourteen Greek churches in New Jersey with two more in the process of organization. In addition there are thirty-one Russian Orthodox churches, sixteen Ukrainian churches (not in communion with Rome), six Carpatho-Russian churches, two Syrian, and

* See Alma White, *The Story of My Life* (4 vols. Zarephath, 1919-1938); and *Looking Back from Beulah* (Zarephath, 1929).

two Serbian churches. Each nationality group has its own bishop, though the diocesan centers for most of them are in New York City. The Carpatho-Russian church was originally a Uniate church in communion with Rome. In 1927, however, it broke away from Roman obedience and became part of the Orthodox family.

The chief problem faced by the Orthodox in establishing their churches was the same one faced by the Roman Catholics a century before: how to overcome the "foreign" label of their communion. Not only were the services held in a foreign tongue, but most of the priests were recent immigrants whose orientation to American life was often quite limited. The children of the immigrants, educated in American schools and wanting to be identified as Americans were apt to cut themselves off from everything relating to the "old country," and this included their church. If the Orthodox church was to survive it had to make itself at home in this country. As long as there was no episcopal control and each priest operated on his own as best he could, the task was impossible. But even when bishops arrived the problem was not solved, because the church needed an adequate supply of American-born priests. These could only be provided if there were schools to train candidates for the priesthood. Gradually, all those difficulties were overcome. Bishops who had been duly consecrated in their national churches came over to lead the congregations of their communion in this country. Then schools were founded. The two most important are Holy Cross Seminary in Brookline, Massachusetts, for the Greek Orthodox and St. Vladimir's Seminary for Russian Orthodox in Yonkers, New York. Today about half of the Orthodox priests in New Jersey are American born.

The next step was to make membership in the Orthodox Church as normal for an American as membership in any other religious body. During the first third of the present century it was an uphill climb with many priests unable to hold their people. But since then the tide has changed. The growing number of American-trained priests has helped. Then, afternoon schools were opened in all parishes to teach children of Greek and Russian parents the elements of their faith as well as something about the history of their church. They also teach Greek and Russian to second-generation children who otherwise might never learn the language in which their liturgy is written. While there is no canon law forbidding the conduct of worship in English, most of the Orthodox churches maintain their services in the traditional tongue. They also have been beneficiaries of the ecumenical movement which has made other Christians concerned to know more about them and which has brought the Orthodox into vital contact with these other Christian traditions.

The traditional divisions of American religious bodies into Protestant, Catholic, and Jewish was always an embarrassment to the Orthodox since they were unable to identify with any one of the three. Even though their numbers were small, they felt that a separate category should be created for them in order to give their members in the Armed Forces adequate spiritual care and to give recognition to their traditional religious festivals. Accordingly, a bill was introduced into the New Jersey Legislature officially recognizing the Orthodox as a fourth major faith. The bill was finally passed and became law in 1955. So the Orthodox secured an identity of their own and also became adjusted to life in America. A measure of their success is shown by the fact that though immigration has slowed to a trickle, the membership of the Orthodox churches continues to grow in the state with reported accessions to their congregations of people who are not of their national background at all.*

The Jews faced much the same problem as the Orthodox. Once the children of the immigrants became Americanized, they tended to regard the worship in the syna-

* Basiliou Th. Zoustis, *The Greek Americans and their Activities: A History of the Greek Archdiocese of North and South America* (in Greek; New York, 1954). Information was also secured from the Reverend Demetrios J. Constantelos of St. Demetrios Greek Orthodox Church, Perth Amboy.

gogue and temple as somehow un-American. Many not only abandoned the faith of their fathers but abandoned religion altogether until a lower percentage of Jews claimed some religious affiliation than any other racial or national group. The creation of the Reform and Conservative branches of Judaism was an attempt to overcome this condition, but as late as 1948 it was estimated that among the 24,500 Jewish families in Essex County alone less than one-third of them provided any religious education for their children.* Since then there has been some improvement in this situation. Most temples and synagogues maintain afternoon schools for religious education, and there are a number of full-time schools for Jewish children, mostly under the auspices of Conservative congregations. In addition the Jewish congregations supported organizations such as the Jewish Chautauqua Society and the B'nai B'rith which serve to promote a better understanding of Judaism by Gentile Americans.

From this account thus far it would appear that the citizens of New Jersey are quite religiously inclined. For a majority this is undoubtedly true. They certainly have a wide variety of religious institutions from which to choose. At the same time there have always been a number, and at times a sizable number, who have shown little if any religious interest at all. It is not very often that indifference has turned into open antagonism, yet there have been instances of this also. Usually it has been related to some form of social doctrine which regards religion as a reactionary influence upon society. It is possible to detect some of this in the first of two Utopian societies that were founded in New Jersey. The North American Phalanx, as it was called, dates back to 1843, when a group of philanthropists including Albert Brisbane, Horace Greeley, and Charles F. Dana helped purchase seven hundred acres of land near Red Bank for the establishment of a communal society. Its organization was based on the social ideas of Charles Fourier, a French

* "Our Life in Our Time," published by the Jewish Community Council of Essex County (Newark, 1948).

economist and philosopher, and it soon became evident that it had very little religious concern. One of its defenders in trying to counter charges of irreligion wrote, "The religious views of a majority of the association might be characterized as liberal; and although there were some who adhered to orthodox forms of worship, yet . . . the associated life tended greatly to modify the asperities of sectarian bigotry." * Even though the Phalanx lasted only thirteen years, about thirty or forty families withdrew from the Phalanx to found a second community, apparently because of the religious issue. One of the dissidents wrote to a friend, "I would advise all persons who have any respect or regard for the religion of the Bible . . . to keep entirely away, at least from the North American Phalanx." ** The new organization which they founded in 1853 was the Raritan Bay Union located at Eagleswood near Perth Amboy. While it was a socialistic experiment it was not irreligious as the preamble to its Constitution made clear:

To establish branches of agriculture and mechanics whereby industry, education and social life may in principle and practice be arranged in conformity to the Christian religion and where all ties . . . which are sanctified by the will of God . . . may be purified and perfected; where the advantages of co-operation may be secured and the evils of competition avoided.†

Even though there were a number of famous names associated with the Union such as Theodore Weld and James G. Birney, the famous abolitionists, and William Henry Channing, the Unitarian minister, the Union disbanded about the time of the beginning of the Civil War.

* Charles Sears, *The North American Phalanx* (Prescott, Wisconsin, 1886), 12.
** Letter by Eleazer Parmlee quoted by Maude H. Greene, "Raritan Bay Union, Eagleswood, N. J.," *Proceedings of The New Jersey Historical Society*, LXVIII, Nos. 1, 4.
† Maude H. Greene, "Raritan Bay Union, Eagleswood, N. J.," *Proceedings of The New Jersey Historical Society*, LXVIII, Nos. 1, 6.

Another social experiment with a decidedly anti-religious bias was the Modern School located near Stelton. It was the outgrowth of a group, most of whose members were Jewish, known as the Ferrer Colony. They took their name and many of their ideas from a radical Spanish educator, Francisco Ferrer, who was executed in 1909 for alleged complicity in a plot to overthrow the Spanish government. The Modern School was founded in New York City, but when their accommodations became too cramped the Colony purchased a farm in North Stelton and moved the School there in 1915. The purpose of the school was to provide a more radical kind of education for the members of the Colony than the public schools afforded. The ideas on which the school operated were socialist, anarchist, anti-religious, and anti-patriotic in the contemporary meaning of those terms. As one of its quarterly publications expressed it,

Our aim in the Ferrer School is to free both the child and the adult from the false conventionalities and superstitions which now hinder the progress of the race. We believe that these superstitions operate chiefly in the fields of industry, religion and sex, so that we especially direct attention to these three subjects.*

The number of students was never very large, and by the early 1950's it passed out of existence altogether.

MODERNIST-FUNDAMENTALIST DISPUTE

The diversity produced by new church groups and agencies entering the State was increased by at least one church schism in the first half of the century. Radical ideas from Europe, with radical social upheavals at home produced severe tensions within many of the old-line denominations. Most of them finally weathered the storm without internal divisions, but the Presbyterians, who theologically always take themselves very seriously, be-

* *The Modern School*, No. 5 (1913), 6.

came embroiled in a denomination-wide battle which had its storm center on the campus of Princeton Theological Seminary. The dispute between the liberal wing, or modernists as they came to be known, and the conservative wing, or fundamentalists, raged around the question of what are the essential doctrines of the Christian faith. The Presbyterian General Assembly in 1910 defined five doctrines as "essential": the infallibility of Scripture, the Virgin Birth, substitutionary atonement, the bodily resurrection of Christ from the dead, and Christ's miracles. This strict fundamentalist approach was strongly opposed by many of the graduates of Union Seminary in New York who wished more leeway in doctrinal interpretation. The battle was fought on a number of fronts at the same time. The Board of Foreign Missions of the Church came under attack for alleged modernism among some of its missionaries. The Presbytery of New York was charged with allowing a Baptist minister, Harry Emerson Fosdick, to preach modernist sermons in the First Presbyterian Church of New York City. In this dispute the Presbyterians of New Jersey were deeply divided. There were many ministers in the State who in one way or another favored the liberal position. When the 1923 General Assembly voted to order New York Presbytery to correct the preaching of Dr. Fosdick, only 38 per cent of the New Jersey commissioners voted in favor of the motion.*

The division within the Church was reflected in the faculty of the Church's oldest seminary at Princeton. Without exception they were all theologically conservative, but whereas a group led by Dr. J. Gresham Machen, believed that the Church should drive out all liberals, a substantial portion of the faculty came to feel such a militant attitude would do more harm than good. The issue, of course, was more than doctrinal. It revolved around the question of whether the Seminary and the Church it served should be exclusive in its make-up, allowing only one point of view with regard to doctrine,

* See chart on the vote in Lefferts A. Loetscher, *The Broadening Church* (Philadelphia, 1957), 113.

or whether it should be inclusive with both liberal and conservative positions permitted in its membership. It was not until 1929 that the issue was resolved by the reorganization of the Seminary, granting increased powers to the board of trustees and the president. It was a victory for the inclusive party, but it was not without cost. The conservative members of the Princeton faculty withdrew and organized the Westminster Theological Seminary in Philadelphia. In turn they led to a withdrawal from the Presbyterian Church of over one hundred ministers who organized themselves as the Orthodox Presbyterian Church. Considering all the bitterness and recrimination which these proceedings entailed, it is significant that those who withdrew to form the Orthodox Presbyterian Church were few in number, and that Church has not grown much since.*

INTER-CHURCH COOPERATION

From this brief examination of the first three decades in the religious life of twentieth century New Jersey it would appear that the dominant note was diversity and disunity. Such a judgment, while superficially true, ignores a much more important development that was taking place. Even before this period there were quiet but persistent movements toward unity which affected nearly all the religious bodies of the State. As churchmen tried to devise ways to overcome the rising spirit of secularism and the challenge posed by social vices and inequities they found themselves thrown together in various common tasks. At first it was the Protestant Christians who were chiefly involved, but later both Catholics and Jews were drawn into ecumenical activities. Since it has already been a peculiar tenet of American Protestantism that nearly all problems will find their solution through individual conversion, it is not surprising that one of the earliest agencies to promote unity was the evangelistic campaign. When Dwight L. Moody and Ira

* For a detailed discussion of the Presbyterian conflict see Lefferts A. Loetscher, *The Broadening Church* (Philadelphia, 1957).

D. Sankey held their great revival services in New York and Philadelphia during the winter of 1875-1876, thousands of New Jersey citizens went to the services. The same was true during Billy Sunday's Philadelphia campaign of 1915. Meanwhile lesser-known evangelists crisscrossed the state holding their services in any community which sought their leadership. The length of each campaign depended upon the response which the community gave. As long as the preacher had a "full house" the services were apt to continue. At times they lasted a month and a half as occurred when the Reverend George Wood Anderson conducted tent services in New Brunswick in 1917,* though more frequently they resembled the two-week revival such as the one held by an evangelist named B. Fay Mills in Elizabeth.** In these campaigns the Protestant churches of the local community cooperated in organizing and supporting the venture, in the hope, no doubt, that the membership of local churches would increase as a result. More often than not, the chief advantage which accrued was a greater cordiality of the various cooperating churches toward each other.†

Another important source of unity was the involvement of churchmen in a wide variety of benevolent enterprises of a non-demoninational nature. One of the earliest of these was the temperance movement which began as a result of the preaching of Anthony Benezet, the Quaker, and the writing of Benjamin Rush, the Philadelphia doctor. Soon it absorbed the energy of the women, especially, from many different denominations. Beginning with the "Sober Society" founded in Allentown, New Jersey, 1805,‡ it spread over the state with

* *New Brunswick Daily Home News,* January 1 to February 12, 1917.

** "The Story of a Revival: a Narrative of the Mills Meetings held in Elizabeth, N. J., 1892," (Special Collections Department, Rutgers University Library).

† See William G. McLoughlin, Jr., *Modern Revivalism: Charles G. Finney to Billy Graham* (New York, 1959).

‡ See *Proceedings of The New Jersey Historical Society,* XIV, No. 3, 334-336.

temperance organizations appearing in nearly every large city as well as in many small ones. The American Bible Society was another inter-denominational agency which secured the support of Protestant churchmen regardless of sect or creed. One of the men chiefly responsible for the formation of this Society was Elias Boudinot of Burlington, the organizer and first president of the New Jersey Bible Society. He was instrumental in gaining the consent of the Bible Societies of New York and Philadelphia to join with the New Jersey Society in forming the American Bible Society. Boudinot was elected the first president of the national organization in 1816, and he served in this capacity until his death in 1821. Later in the nineteenth century the Young Men's Christian Association and the Young Women's Christian Association enlisted the cooperation of many churches.

Perhaps the most important of these agencies, however, was the New Jersey Sunday School Association. From the very beginning the Sunday School movement was a powerful agency for church extension and the training of the young, though the churches looked on the movement with suspicion at first as being a British import which patriotic Americans could well do without. Despite that fact, individual Sunday Schools were started near the end of the eighteenth century in both Philadelphia and New York. The first such school in New Jersey appears to be the one begun by Sarah Colt, the daughter of a cotton-factory owner in Paterson. In 1794 she opened a school for the children of the factory workers in the city. Other early schools on Sunday were started at Swedesboro in 1809, at New Brunswick in 1811, and at Newark in 1813.* In 1817 the Philadelphia societies joined to form the Sunday and Adult School Union, and seven years later the New York schools came into the Union which was renamed the American Sunday School

---

* *Encyclopedia of Sunday Schools and Religious Education,* I, 279; Erna Hardt, "Christian Education in New Jersey" (Unpublished doctoral dissertation, School of Education, New York University), 159-166.

Union.* The first report of that Union in 1825 noted that already New Jersey had 46 auxiliaries in the Union which included well over one hundred Sunday Schools. In the quaint wording of the report, one of the schools in Newark told that "within the last six months, twenty-five teachers and twenty scholars have become hopefully pious." **

In time the opposition of the churches turned to enthusiastic support, as the Sunday Schools proved to be a powerful means for evangelism and religious education of the young. The rapid growth of the movement in New Jersey is shown by the fact that in 1826 there were 293 schools with 307 recorded the following year.† In 1858 the various New Jersey schools and auxiliaries met in New Brunswick for a state-wide convention which led to the formation of the New Jersey Sunday School Association. Without a doubt this was the most important unitive influence among New Jersey Protestant churches in the nineteenth century. Each year the representatives of Sunday Schools from churches all over the State met to share experiences and learn from one another. Out of this grew the famous Methods School, a six-weeks training program for Sunday School teachers and superintendents, and the first summer school of its kind ever held in the United States. Beginning in 1894 it met first of all in Library Hall at Asbury Park. When it outgrew those quarters, the school was moved to the Blair Academy in 1924 where it remained until it was suspended in 1942 due to declining enrollments and the dislocations produced by World War II. It was in 1924 at Burlington that the Association changed its name and enlarged its sphere of activities. Thereafter it was called the New Jersey Council of Religious Education.

The Sunday School movement in New Jersey, which

* E. Morris Fergusson, *Historic Chapters in Christian Education in America* (New York, 1935), 14-22.
** *First Report of the American Sunday-School Union,* 1825, p. 9.
† *Second Report of the American Sunday-School Union,* 10; *Third Report of the American Sunday-School Union,* 7.

led up to the creation of the Council, was one of the most creative enterprises of its kind in America. Even a partial list of its innovations makes an impressive display. The first Infant-School Teachers' Association for Sunday School work was formed in Newark in 1870. The Cradle Roll idea began in Elizabeth in 1877. Out of the Methods School referred to above came a number of improvements which subsequently influenced church schools all over the country. The Graded Lesson plans which were approved by the International Sunday School Convention in 1902 were first outlined at the Asbury Park School in 1896. One of the earliest laboratory experiments in vacation church schools was held at the same place in 1925. Altogether, the imagination and insight provided by Sunday School teachers and leaders in New Jersey enriched Protestant churches all over the world.* Another innovation closely related to the church school was the inauguration in 1866 of Children's Day. Shortly after beginning their pastorate at the Trinity Methodist Church of Merchantville, the Reverend and Mrs. R. S. Harris lost their only child by pneumonia. To honor their boy, they planned a church service in which the children of the congregation had the primary part. It was such a success that it became in time a traditional service for the congregation, and the practice spread to other churches across the State. Today it has become a national observance for many denominations.**

The next important step in Protestant inter-church relationships was the creation in 1935 of the New Jersey State Council of Churches. It grew out of a need on the part of the major denominations to pool their influence in combatting some of the social problems which Christians were encountering in the State. The mobility of population which tended to undercut the stability of the

* Erna Hardt, "Christian Education in New Jersey" (Unpublished doctoral dissertation, School of Education, New York University), 428 f.

** Frank B. Stanger, *The Methodist Trail in New Jersey* (Camden, 1961), 47.

local congregation, the need for legislative action with regard to decent housing, schooling, and honesty in public office made common action appear not only advisable but necessary. When World War II broke out, the State Council set up a Commission on War Emergency Services which supported Protestant representatives at Camp Dix, Camp Kilmer, and other military installations throughout the State. They cooperated with chaplains to meet the religious needs of the men in the armed forces. Meanwhile local councils of churches sprang up in all the major cities of the State until today there is scarcely a hamlet or town with four or more Protestant churches that does not boast a local ministerium or council of churches. The movement toward greater organizational cooperation was at high tide. It was finally culminated in 1945, just at the end of the war, when three inter-church organizations, the New Jersey State Council of Churches, the Council of Religious Education, and the United Council of Church Women of New Jersey merged to form the New Jersey Council of Churches.* The Council which was incorporated in 1950 is the most effective agency for Protestant corporate action in the State today. Even though it represents only 15 denominations, those denominations include more than 80 per cent of the Protestant communicant membership in the State. While the Council does not pretend to speak for all the membership of its constituent denominations, it does involve them in a wide circle of common concerns and thereby helps to bring about effective action.

The dimensions of this concern are made evident from the departments into which the Council is organized. The Department of College and University Ministries involves the church in the campus life of the colleges and universities of the State. Campus chaplains seek to relate students to local churches and also give them opportunities through seminars and discussion groups to relate their intellectual adventure to their faith. A very differ-

* The minutes recording the history of the merger are deposited in the Library of Bloomfield College, Bloomfield.

ent kind of ministry is supplied by the Department of Institutional Ministries which seeks to provide a spiritual guidance to individuals in state penal and correctional institutions, hospitals, and similar agencies for the insane or addicted patient. It also provides assistance to local councils of churches in serving the religious needs of hospitals in their area. The Radio and Television Department explores ways whereby the churches may use more effectively these mass media of communication. Legislative concerns are studied by the Department of Social Education and Action, while the needs of migrant labor are studied and met through the activities of the Department of Work Among Migrants. The Research and Church Development Department conducts demographic studies to project the needs of the church in the future, and the Department of United Church Women sponsors the World Day of Prayer and seeks to mobilize Christian women for more effective witness to their Lord.* The mere enumeration of these activities testifies to the wide areas in which cooperation among local churches is possible and where experience already shows them to be highly effective.

It is not surprising, then, to discover that the New Jersey churches have been enthusiastic participants in various attempts to bring about church union. Two world wars with their attendant dislocations encouraged cooperative efforts among the churches which in turn inspired the movement toward unity at the congregational level. An interesting example of this occurred in New Brunswick during 1917 and 1918. Four of the churches in the community representing the Dutch Reformed, the Presbyterian, and the Episcopal denominations began holding union evening services to pray for the men in service and the successful termination of the war. They felt a close kinship already for their congregations could trace an unbroken history back to the

* See *Nineteenth Annual Meeting of the General Assembly, New Jersey Council of Churches* (Mimeographed report at the Council office in East Orange).

early eighteenth century. As the result of their common services and a desire to do something constructive to forward unity they formed a united committee to approach the Reformed Classis, the Presbyterian Presbytery, and the Episcopal bishop, the Right Reverend Paul Matthews, with a plan which would lead to inter-communion and a complete reciprocity of ministries in the four congregations. The plan, which was worked out by the four ministers and lay representatives of the four churches, stipulated that a minister to be chosen by the Classis of New Brunswick would be consecrated a bishop by one or more bishops of the Episcopal Church, and that thereafter he would conduct a service "of mutual commission and recognition for the ministers of the petitioning congregations, in the spirit of the action of the Church at Antioch recorded in Acts 13:3; *such service to contain all elements necessary to the full and free interchange and exercise of ministerial functions in the several congregations by all the pastors.*" (Italics in original) * When the suggested plan reached the higher judicatories it was either buried in committee or politely ignored.

Admittedly, it was ahead of its time, but the quest for unity became stronger with the passing years. The social upheavals which succeeded the First World War, the attempt to make prohibition work, the great depression of the 1930's, the New Deal, all these produced social changes which made religious people of all faiths give a critical look at their denominational allegiance and ask if all the diversity in churches was necessary. The first great denomination to overcome its divisions was the Methodist Church. The schism left by the Civil War and the much earlier separation of the Methodist Protestant branch were still unresolved, though earnest negotiation had been carried on intermittently since the turn of the century. Several times the proposal to unite seemed within reach of success. Once it was put to the vote in 1926 and was turned down by the southern church. Yet

* *The Movement for Church Unity in New Brunswick, N. J.* (New Brunswick, 1918), 9.

the advocates of unity refused to give up, and negotiation continued until 1939 when the long-awaited union was consummated.* No doubt Francis Asbury would have been very pleased. This was but the first of a number of great denominational unions which followed. In 1957 there came into being a new denomination, the United Church of Christ, which was itself the product of two previous smaller mergers. The Congregational Church joined with the Christian Church in 1931 to form the Congregational-Christian Church. Three years later two predominantly German churches merged to create the Evangelical and Reformed Church. Both of these new union churches then united to form the United Church of Christ. This was a particularly significant marriage because for the first time churches with a congregational polity were wedded to churches with a presbyterian polity. If successful, this venture opens all sorts of ecumenical possibilities for the future. Not to be outdone, the Presbyterian Church in the U.S.A. joined forces with the United Presbyterian Church of North America in 1958 to form the United Presbyterian Church in the U.S.A. The latest union brought together three large Lutheran Synods in 1962 to form the Lutheran Church in America, the largest body of Lutherans in the western world.

The effect of these unions upon New Jersey churchmen at first appeared to be slight. Some congregations had to change their names. The bounds of local judicatories were changed slightly, but life went on pretty much the same at the local level. Yet in a deeper sense there was a profound change brought about by these unions. The old New York–Philadelphia axis which bulked so large in the denominational histories of the eighteenth and nineteenth centuries now was overshadowed by much broader patterns of church life. And as a result New Jersey emerged with a church life of its own independent of the urban centers at its northern and southern extremi-

* See James H. Straughn, *Inside Methodist Union* (Nashville, 1958).

ties. This is illustrated by the action of the Holy See in establishing Newark as a Roman Catholic archdiocese in 1937 covering the whole state. Three suffragan sees, Camden, Paterson, and Trenton, were created answerable to Archbishop Thomas J. Walsh in Newark. Thus the Catholics in New Jersey were now independent of both Philadelphia and New York for the first time. The two million five hundred thousand members claimed by the Catholic church in New Jersey make it by far the largest religious body in the State. In only three counties, Sussex, Ocean, and Salem, do they not constitute the largest denomination, and in many of the more populous counties they constitute more than 50 per cent of the citizenry.* This has raised questions and fears among Protestants regarding the political power represented by this majority.

Be that as it may, two factors have intervened to allay at least some of the fears. One of these is the growing evidence that Catholic majorities will not always vote as a bloc. On local issues, such as a school bond issue, Catholic majorities have voted for a new public school even though to do so increased the difficulty of the parochial school system. On national issues as well there were many Catholics who refused to vote for the first Catholic presidential candidate. The second factor is the influence of the late pontiff, Pope John XXIII. In the space of his five-year reign he did more to create a cordial atmosphere between Roman Catholics and other Christians than any other pontiff since the sixteenth century. Particularly since the Ecumenical Council which Pope John convened in 1962, the inter-church relations have become noticeably more cordial. Since immigration now has tapered off, it no longer threatens the balance among religious bodies. Religious diversity within the State is still the dominant characteristic of church life, but within this diversity denominations have learned to live more or less at peace.

* Edwin S. Gaustad, *Historical Atlas of Religion in America* (New York, 1962), endpaper.

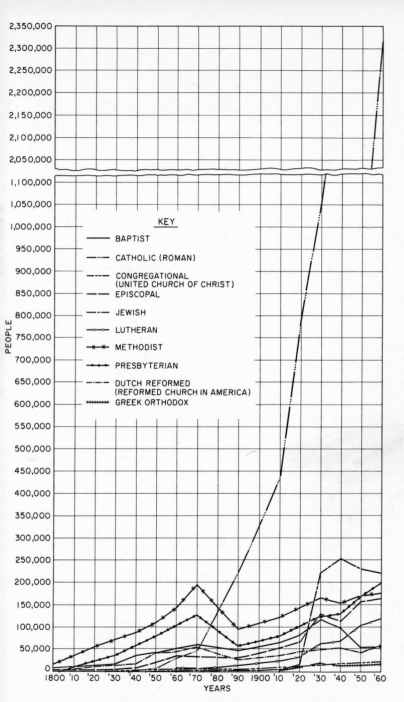

RELATIVE GROWTH OF CHURCHES IN NEW JERSEY,
1800-1960
The figures on which this chart is based are a combination of
United States census lists and denominational statistics. They
must be considered only approximations.

In the First Presbyterian and Trinity Church of South Orange there is a stained-glass window which may serve as a symbol of religion in New Jersey today. A number of years ago a group of Jews in South Orange wished to form a local congregation. Not having a place to worship or the funds to build one, they sought and secured permission from the session of the First Church to hold a Friday night service in their building. After a time the Jewish congregation purchased the house of a wealthy antiques dealer with the intention of turning it into a Jewish temple. The house had been fitted with a number of *objets d'art* by its former owner, among which was a magnificent stained-glass window of the Virgin Mary being adored by Louis IX of France before he led his army on the Crusade to the Holy Land. The window was obviously inappropriate for a Jewish temple, and since the motif was Christian the Jews conceived the idea of donating the window as an expression of thanks to the Presbyterian Church. A suitable plaque was prepared which reads, "This window has been presented to the First Presbyterian Church of the Oranges and Maplewood by Temple Israel of the Oranges and Maplewood in recognition of the friendship, mutual appreciation, and good will which exists between these two congregations." Here is a Protestant Church with a Roman Catholic window presented by a Jewish congregation! Unusual as this is, it stands as a fitting symbol of the way the religious diversity in New Jersey provides both variety and enrichment to the people of the State.

In 1676 William Penn wrote a letter to those families who planned to settle in the newly-purchased proprietary of West Jersey. He was concerned that his colony be grounded on religious principles and that the inhabitants learn to live together in peace. His words, though couched in antique phraseology, are still worth remembering:

Be it known unto you all, in the name and fear of Almighty God, his glory and honour, power and wisdom, truth and kingdom, is dearer to us than all visible things; and as our eye has been single, and our heart sincere to the living God, in this as in other things; so we desire all whom it may concern, that all groundless jealousies may be judged down and watched against, and that all extremes may be avoided on all hands by the power of the Lord; that nothing which hurts or grieves the holy life of truth in any that goes or stays, may be adhered to; nor any provocations given to break precious unity.*

Even though Penn's counsel has been repeatedly ignored, it is still the best guide for a religious people who worship their God in diverse ways and have learned to practice forbearance and respect toward one another in doing so.

* Quoted in Samuel Smith, *The History of the Colony of Nova-Caesarea, or New Jersey* (2nd ed; Burlington, 1877), 91.

BIBLIOGRAPHICAL NOTE

Sources for the study of religion in New Jersey are scattered widely across the State. Especially fine collections of primary source materials are located in the library of The New Jersey Historical Society (230 Broadway, Trenton, New Jersey), the Special Collections Section of Rutgers University Library, Princeton University Library, Drew University Library, and the Gardner A. Sage Library of New Brunswick Theological Seminary. The following brief selection of titles is designed to assist the reader who would like to pursue in more detail some subject of particular interest.

A wealth of background material is contained in the *Proceedings of The New Jersey Historical Society*, the *Geneological Magazine of New Jersey*, and the *Journal of the Presbyterian Historical Society*. Each of these publications has an annual index which guides the reader to relevant articles. Under the Works Progress Administration the Government subsidized inventories of the church archives in New Jersey which were published in mimeographed form. Unfortunately, *The Historical Records Survey: Inventory of the Church Archives of New Jersey* was not completed, but before the project ended, inventories were published on *Baptist Bodies,* (1938), a *Seventh Day Baptist Supplement* (1939), *Baha'i Assemblies* (1940), *Congregational Christian Churches,* (1941), *The Evangelical Church* (1941), *Presbyterians* (1940), *Protestant Episcopal Church* (1940), and *Unitarians* (1940). For a general treatment of religion in New Jersey, see William T. Hanzsche, "The History of the Churches in New Jersey" in Vol. II, *The Story of New Jersey* (5 vols.; New York, 1945). A very valuable study of relative denominational growth with brief histories of the churches is found in Edwin S. Gaustad, *Historical Atlas of Religion in America* (New York, 1962).

Religion in Colonial New Jersey is treated in a scholarly fashion by John E. Pomfret in two volumes, *The Province of West New Jersey 1609-1702*. (Princeton, 1956) and *The Province of East New Jersey 1609-1702* (Princeton, 1962). They are well documented and have good bibliographies. A much older book, but still useful because of the letters, laws, and other primary sources quoted extensively in it, is Samuel Smith, *The History of the Colony of Nova-Caesarea, or New Jersey* (Burlington, 1877). Among the studies of the various early settlements in the Colony the Swedes are covered by Amandus Johnson in *The Swedish Settlements on the Delaware, 1638-1664* (2 vols.; New York, 1902). The classic study of the Friends is by Rufus M. Jones, *The Quakers in the American Colonies* (London, 1911), and a later work which is also valuable is Sydney E. Fisher, *The Quaker Colonies: a Chronicle of the Proprietors of the Delaware* (New Haven, 1921). The definitive work on the Anglicans is written by Nelson R. Burr, *The Anglican Church in New Jersey* (Philadelphia, 1954), who also wrote another valuable study, *Education in New Jersey 1630-1871* (Princeton, 1942). Congregational and Presbyterian beginnings are treated by Joseph Atkinson in *The History of Newark, New Jersey* (Newark, 1878). A very valuable study based on original sources is the article by Nelson Burr in two successive issues of *Proceedings of The New Jersey Historical Society*, "The Religious History of New Jersey Before 1702," LVI, Nos. 3 and 4. Especially helpful is the map accompanying this article, which locates the first churches and religious settlements in New Jersey.

For anyone wishing to become better acquainted with New Jersey in the first half of the eighteenth century there is a wealth of letters, diaries, and memoirs available. Representative of these are *The Journal and Letters of Francis Asbury* (3 vols.; London, 1958), George Whitefield's *Journals* (London, 1960), John Woolman's *Journal* (Boston, 1871), and the *Memoirs of the Rev. David Brainerd, Missionary to the Indians* by Jonathan Edwards (New Haven, 1822). The *Sermons* of Theodorus Jacobus Frelinghuysen, translated and edited by William Demarest (New York, 1856), give a good example of Calvinistic preaching in the colony. The *Ecclesiastical Records of the State of New York* (7 vols.; 1901-1916) give a contemporary account of the growing pains of the Dutch Reformed Church along the Raritan. The best history of the Dutch Church during this period is contained in *A Manual of the Reformed Church in America*, edited by Edward T. Corwin (4th ed.; New York, 1902). Baptist records are contained in *Minutes of the Philadelphia Baptist Association from A.D. 1707 to A.D. 1807* (Philadelphia, 1851) and the invaluable two-volume work by Morgan Edwards, *Materials Toward a History of the Baptists* (Philadelphia, 1792). Henry C. Vedder has also given us a useful account in his *History of the Baptists in the Middle States* (Philadelphia, 1898).

Among the many studies of early Presbyterianism in New Jersey the most recent scholarly work is *The Formation of an American Tradition* by Leonard J. Trinterud (Philadelphia, 1949). An older book which is still valuable was written by Charles A. Briggs, *American Presbyterianism, its Origin and Early History* (New York, 1885). *The Memoirs of the Reverend William Tennent, formerly of Freehold, N. J.* edited by Elias Boudinot (Newark, 1834) is a valuable early source, as is *The Days of Makemie; or, the Vine Planted,* by L. B. Bowen (Philadelphia, 1885). Archibald Alexander recorded the activity of the Presbyterians during the Great Awakening in his *Biographical Sketches of the Founder and Principal Alumni of the Log College Together with an Account of the Revivals of Religion Under their Ministry,* (Princeton, 1845). A broader treatment of the same period is found in Charles H. Maxson's *The Great Awakening in the Middle Colonies* (Chicago, 1920).

Early memories of New Jersey Methodism are recorded in two volumes by George A. Raybold, *Annals of Methodism* (Philadelphia, 1847) and *Reminiscences of Methodism in West Jersey* (New York, 1849). In a somewhat similar rambling style, John Atkinson wrote *Memorials of Methodism in New Jersey* (2nd ed.; Philadelphia, 1860) and *A Centennial History of American Methodism* (New York, 1884). William L. Duren's biography, *Francis Asbury: Founder of American Methodism and Unofficial Minister of State* (New York, 1928) is a readable account of the first American Methodist bishop. An excellent background source which provides local color for this period is Andrew D. Mellick, Jr.'s book, *The Story of an Old Farm or Life in New Jersey in the Eighteenth Century* (Somerville, 1889).

One of the best introductions to the role of New Jersey during the Revolutionary War is Leonard Lundin's *Cockpit of the Revolution: the War for Independence in New Jersey*

(Princeton, 1940). Additional material is found in the first volume of *A History of Trenton,* published under the auspices of the Trenton Historical Society (2 vols.; Princeton, 1929). The religious background is discussed in William W. Sweet's *Religion in the Development of American Culture* (New York, 1952). The Reverend Abraham Messler wrote down little vignettes of life in the Raritan Valley during the Revolution in his *First Things in Old Somerset* (Somerville, 1899). Aside from previous works already cited, the biography, *President Witherspoon,* by Varnum L. Collins (2 vols.; Princeton, 1925) is the best source for a study of Presbyterian involvement in the Revolution. The problems confronted by the Anglicans are treated in three scholarly books: Arthur L. Cross, *The Anglican Episcopate and the American Colonies* (New York, 1902), Carl Bridenbaugh, *Mitre and Sceptre* (New York, 1962), and James T. Addison, *The Episcopal Church in the United States* (New York, 1951). The roots of the earliest American schism in the Methodist Church are traced by Ancel H. Bassett, *A Concise History of the Methodist Protestant Church from its Origin* (Pittsburgh, 1882). The best source for a history of early Lutheranism in New Jersey is Henry Melchior Muhlenberg's *Journals* (3 vols.; Philadelphia, 1942-1958) which have scattered references to visits to Lutheran congregations along the Raritan. Prof. Norman H. Maring of Eastern Baptist Seminary has written the most recent as well as the most thorough *History of New Jersey Baptists* though it is as yet unpublished. The manuscript is in the possession of the New Jersey Baptist Convention in East Orange. Roman Catholic beginnings are recorded in John G. Shea, *A History of the Catholic Church Within the Limits of the United States* (2 vols.; New York, 1890) and John T. Ellis, *American Catholicism* (Chicago, 1956).

Though the sources for Lutheran growth in the mid-nineteenth century are sparse for New Jersey, mention of it is made in Abdel R. Wentz, *A Basic History of Lutheranism in America* (Philadelphia, 1955). There is much more material on the Quakers because of the controversies which brought splits to that communion. Elbert Russell's *History of Quakerism* (New York, 1942) illuminates the causes of the struggle, while Bliss Forbush contributes the biography of *Elias Hicks: Quaker Liberal* (New York, 1956). *The Hicksite Quakers and their Doctrines* (New York, 1897) are described by James De Garmo.

The other divisive figure among New Jersey Friends was Joseph Gurney whose *Memoirs of Joseph John Gurney with Selections from his Journal and Correspondence* (2 vols.; Philadelphia, 1854) provide valuable source material for the schism which he finally caused. A useful biography of the man is *Joseph John Gurney: Banker, Reformer and Quaker* (Middletown, Conn., 1962) by David E. Swift.

One of the best sources for the Protestant Episcopal Church in the State during the first half of the nineteenth century is *The Life and Writings of George Washington Doane* (4 vols.; New York, 1860-1861). Robert S. Bosher's *The American Church and the Formation of the Anglican Communion 1823-1853* (Evanston, Ill., 1962) fills in the details. Methodist growth during this period is best illustrated by C. A. Malmsbury's *Life, Labors, and Sermons of Rev. Charles Pitman, D.D., of the New Jersey Conference* (Philadelphia, 1887). The split in the church brought on by slavery is recounted by John N. Norwood, *The Schism in the Methodist Episcopal Church, 1844: a Study of Slavery and Ecclesiastical Politics* (New York, 1923). Sources on the Presbyterian New School–Old School schism include E. H. Gillett, *History of the Presbyterian Church in the U.S.A.* (2 vols.; Philadelphia, 1864) and Isaac V. Brown, *A Historical Vindication of the Abrogation of the Plan of Union by the Presbyterian Church in the U.S.A.* (Philadelphia, 1855) representing the Old-School view. The New-School view is reflected in Edward D. Morris, *A Book of Remembrance: The Presbyterian Church New School 1837-1869: An Historical Review* (Columbus, Ohio, 1905), Zebulon Crocker, *The Catastrophe of the Presbyterian Church in 1837, Including a full view of the Recent Theological Controversies in New England* (New Haven, 1838), and Samuel J. Baird, *A History of the New School and of the Questions Involved in the Disruption of the Presbyterian Church in 1838* (Philadelphia, 1868).

Representative of the literature that grew out of the slavery controversy are John Henry Hopkins, *A Scriptural, Ecclesiastical, and Historical View of Slavery from the Days of the Patriarch Abraham to the Nineteenth Century* (New York, 1864); J. B. Dobbins, *The Bible Against Slavery: a Vindication of the Sacred Scriptures Against the Charge of Authorizing Slavery, A Reply to Bishop Hopkins* (Philadelphia, 1864); and Henry S. Cooley, *A Study of Slavery in New Jersey* (Baltimore,

1896). The Civil War is treated in John Y. Foster, *New Jersey and the Rebellion* (Newark, 1868); Lemuel Moss, *Annals of the United States Christian Commission* (Philadelphia, 1868); and H. Clay Trumbull, *War Memories of an Army Chaplain* (New York, 1898).

Details on the rapid growth of the Catholic Church in New Jersey may be found in Joseph M. Flynn, *The Catholic Church in New Jersey* (Morristown, 1904) which consists chiefly of short parish histories, and Sister M. Hildegarde Yaeger's *Life of James Roosevelt Bayley, First Bishop of Newark and Eighth Archbishop of Baltimore* (Washington, 1947). General studies of Jewish growth are found in Nathan Glazer, *American Judaism* (Chicago, 1957) and Peter Wiernik, *History of the Jews in America: from the Period of the Discovery of the New World to the Present Time* (2nd ed.; New York, 1931). More specialized studies are found in Albert M. Friedenberg, "The Jews of New Jersey from the Earliest Times to 1850," *Publications of the American Jewish Historical Society*, XVII (1909); Philip R. Goldstein, *Social Aspects of the Jewish Colonies of South Jersey* (New York, 1921); and Joshua O. Haberman, "The Jews in New Jersey" (Unpublished MS in Rutgers University Library).

Presbyterian history is dealt with in *Presbyterian Reunion: a Memorial Volume 1837-1871* (New York, 1870) which evaluates the reasons for the healing of the New School–Old School schism, and in Lefferts A. Loetscher, *The Broadening Church: a Study of Theological Issues in the Presbyterian Church since 1869* (Philadelphia, 1857), an especially good treatment of the theological divisions in the Church. E. Clowes Chorley gives a good treatment of the issues contained in the Reform Episcopal schism in his *Men and Movements in the American Episcopal Church* (Hampden, Conn., 1961), while *The Methodist Trail in New Jersey*, edited by Frank B. Stanger (Camden, 1961) gives a somewhat superficial treatment of Methodist growth in this period.

Information on the growth of some sects in New Jersey may be gleaned from their journals and annual reports such as the *Christian Science Journal, the Yearbook of the Seventh Day Adventist Denomination,* and releases from the Watchtower Bible and Tract Society of New York. The story of the Adventist parochial schools is contained in Derrel K. Smith's "Record of the Seventh-Day Adventist Church Schools in New Jersey from their Beginning in 1908 to 1961" (Master's thesis, Princeton Theological Seminary, 1962). A history of the Pillar of Fire sect is found in two works by the founder, Alma White: *Looking Back from Beulah* (Zarephath, 1929) and *The Story of My Life and the Pillar of Fire* (4 vols.; Zarephath, 1919-1938). A sketch of the Greek Orthodox Church is contained in Basiliou Th. Zoustis, *The Greek Americans and their Activities: a History of the Greek Archdiocese of North and South America* (New York, 1954). Brief mention is made of New Jersey Unitarians and Universalists in J. H. Allen and Richard Eddy, *A History of the Unitarians and the Universalists in the United States* (New York, 1894).

The best treatment of the Sunday School movement in New Jersey is contained in Erna Hardt, "Christian Education in New Jersey: a History of Protestant Cooperative Religious Education in the State, its Origin, Development, and Relationship to Other Movements of the Times" (Doctoral dissertation, School of Education, New York University, 1951). A valuable account is *Fifty Years of Progress in the Work of the New Jersey Sunday School Association With a Reprint of the First Report, 1858* (Newark, 1908). An account of the events leading up to the reunion of the Methodist Church North and South and the Methodist Protestant Church is contained in James H. Straughn, *Inside Methodist Union* (Nashville, 1958).

INDEX

Presbyterian Review, 130
Presbytery, 35-37, 39-42, 82-84, 96, 128, 150, 158
Princeton, 41, 52, 58, 60, 64, 83, 84, 93, 96, 97, 106, 128-130, 136, 140, 150, 151, 163
Princeton Theological Seminary, 84, 96, 97, 128-130, 140, 150, 151, 169
Printz, Governor Johan, 8
Proprietors, 3, 10, 25, 29, 164
Protestant, 6, 77, 105, 108, 110-112, 115, 116, 118, 119, 126-129, 134-137, 146, 151, 153, 155, 156, 160, 161, 169
Pryde, George S., 18
Puritan, 3, 4, 9, 14-17, 34-36

Quaker, 3-6, 8, 10-15, 17, 18, 24, 26-29, 46, 48-51, 57, 63, 67-69, 87-90, 99, 104, 134, 152, 164, 166, 167
Quarterly Meeting, 13, 14, 19, 49, 51
Queen's College, 79

Raccoon, 8
Rahway, 2
Rancocas Valley, 49
Raritan, 2, 17, 18, 31, 32, 34, 56, 61, 80, 81, 86, 164, 166
Raritan Bay Union, 148
Raybold, George A., 165
Red Bank, 147
Reform, 49, 126, 128, 147
Reformed Church in America, 86, 158, 165; *see also* Dutch Reformed
Reformed Episcopal, 131, 132, 168
Revival, Revivalism, 4, 38, 40, 42, 43, 46, 52, 90, 96, 143, 152, 165
Revolutionary War, 18, 34, 48, 52, 54, 57-72, 74, 79, 81-84, 86, 93, 98, 165, 166

Rhode Island, 2, 4, 19, 24, 53
Rhode Island College, 53
Richards, S. H., 8
Ridgewood, 135
Roberts, William, 95
Robertson, Nemi, 138
Roman Catholic, 6, 81, 82, 90, 111-121, 127, 129, 134, 137, 145, 146, 151, 160, 161, 166, 168
Romeyn, Dirck, 61
Rosenhayn, 123
Rowland, John, 40
Ruff, Daniel, 67
Rush, Benjamin, 152
Russell, Elbert, 89, 166
Russian, 122, 144, 146
Russian Orthodox, 144, 145
Rutgers, Henry, 79
Rutgers College, 79, 163
Rutherford, 135

St. Augustine's College, 109
St. Raphael Society, 120
St. Vladimir's Seminary, 145
Salem, 8, 12-14, 18, 81, 160
Salvation Army, 136
San Francisco, 95
Sankey, Ira D., 151, 152
Sargent, Winthrop, 65
Schenck, G. C., 70
Schism, 6, 27, 34, 37, 40, 43, 45, 46, 75, 80, 87, 89, 97, 104, 106, 108, 127, 128, 130-133, 142, 149, 158, 166-168
Schmidt, Hubert, 99, 101, 102
Schneider, Theodore, 81
Schools, 5, 22, 37, 39, 42, 80, 84, 100, 109, 111, 115, 133, 134, 140, 145-147, 149, 153-156, 160, 169; *see* Education
Scotch Plains, 19, 52
Scots, 3, 17, 18, 24, 26, 35, 37, 42, 55, 58, 61, 62, 73
Scott, Clinton L., 20
Seabury, Samuel, 72, 73

Todd, John A., 62
Tolerance, 4, 11, 18, 54, 81, 162
Tory, 62, 64-67, 69, 74
Toy, Joseph, 47
Tranquility, 140
Trenton, 18, 47, 67, 74, 76, 77, 82, 87, 90, 93, 95, 112, 116, 117, 119-122, 142, 143 160, 163, 166
Trinterud, Leonard J., 31, 60, 83, 165
True Dutch Reformed Church, 80
Trumbull, H. Clay, 107, 168
Trusteeism, 116
Turner, Gordon, 54

Ukrainian Orthodox, 144
Uniate, 145
Union (church), 6, 35, 58, 72, 79, 103, 127, 128, 133, 154, 157-159, 168, 169
Union Seminary, N. Y., 97, 106, 128, 130, 150
Unitarian, 134, 135, 148, 163, 169
United Church of Christ, 159
United Council of Church Women, 156, 157
United States Christian Commission, 107, 108, 168
Universalists, 20, 135, 169

Valley Forge, Pa., 65
Van Dyke, John, 98, 103
Vaughan, Edward, 44
Vedder, Henry C., 53, 134, 165
Vermeule, Cornelius C., 69
Vermont, 104
Vineland, 123, 135
Virginia, 3, 36, 51, 54, 64, 75, 83, 107, 109, 123

Walsh, Thomas J., 160
Washington, D. C., 100, 109, 114, 117, 139

Washington, George, 58, 61, 64, 76, 81
Watchtower Bible and Tract Society, 141, 168
Watchung, 2
Watters, William, 48
Webb, Thomas, 47
Webster, William, 17
Weld, Theodore, 148
Welsh, 3, 19
Wentz, Abdel R., 87, 166
Wesley, Charles, 75
Wesley, John, 47, 66, 67, 74, 75
Wesleyan Methodist, 104, 133
Wesleyan Repository, 77
West Grove, 142
West New Jersey, 1-4, 8, 10-16, 19, 25, 29, 67, 81, 93, 161, 164, 165
West Point, 65
Westminster Standards, 26, 37, 53, 83, 96, 128
Westminster Theological Seminary, 151
Westphalia, 30
Whig, 64, 69
White, Alma, 143, 144, 169
White, Arthur K., 144
White, Ellen Harmon, 139
White, William, 71, 72
Whitefield, George, 34, 38, 40, 45-47, 164
Whitehead, William A., 98
Wiernik, Peter, 123, 168
Wigger, Winand M., 120
Wilbur, John, 89
William and Mary, 73
Williamson, J. G., 101
Wills, Daniel, 12
Wilmington, 8
Winchester, Benjamin, 141
Wise, Isaac Mayer, 126
Witchcraft, 55
Witherspoon, John, 58-60, 64, 65, 83, 166
Woodbine 124, 125
Woodbridge, 16, 17, 24, 34, 36

Woodbury, 104
Woolman, John, 49-51, 99, 164
World Day of Prayer, 157
World War I, 130, 144, 157, 158
World War II, 136, 142, 154, 156, 157
Wynbeek, David, 42

Yaeger, M. Hildegarde, 117, 168

Yale, 17, 42, 60
Yearly Meeting, 14, 27, 68, 88, 89
Young Men's Christian Association, 107, 108, 153
Young Women's Christian Association, 153

Zarephath, 143, 144, 169
Zoustis, Basiliou Th., 146, 169
Zwemer, Samuel, 136

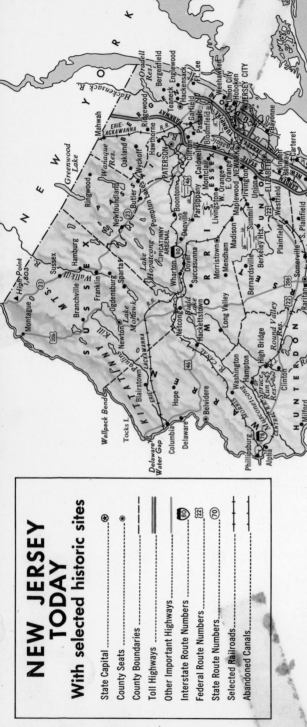

NEW JERSEY TODAY

With selected historic sites

State Capital .... ⊛
County Seats .... ◉
County Boundaries ....
Toll Highways ....
Other Important Highways ....
Interstate Route Numbers 80
Federal Route Numbers 222
State Route Numbers 70
Selected Railroads ....
Abandoned Canals ....

SCALE OF MILES

0   10   20   30   40   50

N